RECKLESS MILLIONAIRE

How to Make Money Online by Developing a **Video Game Mindset**

RENAE CHRISTINE

ISBN: 978-1-953607-23-2 (Hardcover)

Edited by Michael J. Meyer

Printed in the United States of America
10 9 8 7 6 5 4 3 2 1

Dedicated to the Cote family

Thank you for accepting me when you shouldn't have.

CONTENTS

FOREWORD

I remember when I first "ran into" Renae Christine.

Of all places, it was YouTube. Renae commented on a few of my business videos. At the time I didn't think much of it except here is a super-energetic dynamic woman figuring out her business.

Fast forward to years later, I received the now famous "Crying Renae Video" where Renae, quite literally cries her way through the video and shares her story of how she took one of my trainings and made her first $3,000 in sales with her online course and jump started her coaching and mentoring business.

Now? I don't think a week goes by without me telling someone, *"Have you heard of Renae Christine? Do you know her story?"*

Now, on the selfish end, Renae is one of my most successful students who has created a multiple 7-figure empire so I love bragging about her.

But the credit all goes to her. And the amazing brand, business woman and leader she has become.

She is now the leading handmade-to-manufactured business coach worldwide. No doubt on that whatsoever. And she continues to grow.

Renae works hard and smart. Plus she has one of the most LOYAL followings aka "Besties" or "EntreGamers" I've seen online (and I've been involved in online business for over a decade).

Why? Because she really cares. She cares about your success (and she has thousands of success stories to prove it).

Quite simply put…she knows what she is talking about and has a ton to share with you.

Listen to what she says.

Memorize what she says.

Do what she says.

You won't be sorry.

– **David Siteman Garland**
aka DSG CO-Founder Nrdly

CHAPTER 1

Cipher In the Snow

I thought I would be face down in the snow, dead, by the time I hit eleven years old. Each year, my classmates and I watched a movie called "Cipher in the Snow", a BYU special. In it, a depressed, lonely, and neglected kid dies of heart failure after being failed by their parents, classmates, and school system.

Each year that we watched it, an awkward silence would fill the room as the movie ended. I would turn red and just stare at my desk. Even the teacher would be concerned upon looking my way. Why did they do this? Even I knew the answer to that. The kid in the movie resembled how I looked and acted in class. Quiet, depressed, and neglected. My hair was out of control, and I wore tattered clothes with socks designed for a teenage boy. Then, for a few days, my teachers and classmates would feel bad for me. They would tell me to go to the front of the line, ask me to play with them at recess, and even include me by passing me the ball when playing. But it always ended up the same. After a few days, they forgot about the movie. Bullies would then revert to their previous antics. They would spit in my face and physically assault me. One boy kneed me in the back every day as if he were a superhero and I was the villain. All the girls would laugh at me and tease me about my hair, clothes, name, and socks.

This movie and public humiliation repeated every year of grade school. To truly envision me in class, I feel obligated to explain more about my socks, which were likely the biggest problem with my appearance. My parents could not afford to buy me my own pair of socks and I also had three brothers. So, we would share socks out of a 'sock bin'. My parents bought socks for my older brother and threw these socks into the bin. I was instructed to wear them to school. These socks smelled, had holes in them, and were often big enough to go up to my knees but not tight enough to stay up. The socks would float around my ankles. I was quite the sight. In sixth grade, I vividly remember a girl asking me if I was wearing a homeless person's costume for a play I had after school. "Nope," I responded. "These are my real clothes." She felt embarrassed because it was an honest question, and she was not trying to be rude. Yet, even my best friends were cruel to me. They would ask me to play and meet up at their house which was two miles away. Seemed genuine at first. However, when I would arrive, they would refuse to answer the door and I could hear them laughing about it from inside. I would leave and walk back home, only to be tricked by them again the very next day.

So yes, I expected to be just like the kid in the movie and dead by the time I was eleven because everyone around me treated me the same way. Yet I was not the Cipher in the Snow like they believed me to be. In reality, I did not care about having friends, or wearing nice clothes, or even having socks that fit. My mom would have found a way to get me anything I needed had I asked or brought attention to the problem. She knew that I didn't care, and she also likely didn't want to hurt my feelings by telling me that my fashion choices weren't all that great. I didn't care about the bullies enough to tell on them. They were not worth it. They often followed me home from school while laughing at me and spitting on me. I just kept my head down and continued moving forward. I didn't feel bad about myself. I would rightfully understand that those girls were the real losers as I kept my head down to avoid the next spit storm. My little brother was usually across the street walking home with his own set of bullies. Although, he had to use a Blockbuster video backpack, so he got it even worse than me. I heard the Blockbuster video jingle at least 3,000 times that year. "Blockbuster video! Wow! What a difference!"

The truth is though, I was not the Cipher. I just didn't know there was an alternative character to play. I was an entrepreneur. But usually, school counselors do not diagnose anyone with an entrepreneur diagnosis. In thinking, they probably should! It took me thirty-five years to finally diagnose myself with an entrepreneur personality disorder. And it is as extreme as it comes for a diagnosis. No one understands me and I don't understand them...unless they also have the entrepreneur personality disorder, or they are, what I like to call, an Entrevert.

I didn't realize it back then, but that movie could have ended differently. Perhaps it should have. Because what if that kid, instead of dying in the snow, grew up, turned into a superhero, and then became a reckless millionaire? Why couldn't that happen? After all, it happened to me.

And if it happened to me, it could certainly happen to you.

CHAPTER 2

How To Make Money Online Legitimately Without Being Scammed by a Fake Guru

I am going to start off by being brutally honest. The best way to get to a million dollars is to be scammed first. Totally kidding, but if you ask any millionaire if he or she has been scammed, I can almost guarantee that most of them, if not all of them, have been. This is not the end of the world for them, as they have likely learned from their mistakes and implored better strategies in detecting potential future scams.

When I was a single mom with three little children, two of which were still in diapers, I was trying to make money with my 1-year-old YouTube channel…without getting scammed. I really wanted to work from home so I would not have to lose the small apartment where my three kids and I resided. I wanted to be able to support my children to the best of my ability so they would have a happy childhood. I genuinely felt that this would give them a proper chance at life instead of growing up on welfare. The thing is, I was making about a dollar a day with YouTube ads. This meant that I was not able to get my kids clothes or even a cheeseburger from the McDonald's value menu, let alone pay for more expensive items such as glasses or asthma medication. To make matters worse, I felt terrible due to my recent divorce which was my own decision. Now, it did not matter how great of a decision I thought that was at the time. I could have potentially messed up my kids' entire lives if I could not find a way to make money from home. The pressure that I was feeling continued to mount. I felt as though I was a failure as a mom, particularly the time I had to embarrass my eight-year-old daughter when I could not afford to give her five dollars for a class party. The problem was that my bank account was dwindling. I started googling homeless shelters to see what our next options might have to be. This meant that if I did not find a way to make money from home, and quickly, I was going to potentially lose my home, my possessions, and even my own children if the state of Nevada deemed that I could not properly care for them.

Then, something amazing happened...

I decided to stop trying my own way, and instead, bought a $197 course from David Siteman Garland and followed it precisely. The course detailed how to use a specific step by step strategy in a video webinar that helps convert watchers into buyers. It was now crystal clear to me how to perform a proper sales pitch integrated with scarcity in order to get people to check out and purchase a quality product of my own. If this worked,

I could sell anything to anyone at any time. I learned that you cannot just watch free YouTube videos and think you are going to have everything you need to make money online. I tried that desperately for over a year. It clearly was not the answer. Do not assume that the legitimate ways to make money are free on YouTube. Instead, it is essential to buy a legitimate online course from an instructor. As a result of buying this course, I stayed up day and night for two days straight. I then launched a webinar with a sales pitch at the end to a product I thought my audience might like. I was shocked. After the webinar ended, I started seeing sales flood in. Suddenly, I was looking at $1,700 in the bank and my launch was only halfway through. To big entrepreneurs, $1,700 is nothing. To me, it was life. It was oxygen. It was rent. I made a video to David Siteman Garland (DSG) and started crying. I just kept saying "I can't believe it works!" I was astonished. That video is now known as "the infamous crying girl video" by Renae Christine.

This was when I realized that the secret to making money with my 1-year-old YouTube channel was to stop doing things my way and try DSG's way. My plan was to start using this online course for everything I could possibly sell with my skills. I started making a paid membership website. Then I sold it. Made money. But we did not stop there. We then made a website building service. Then we sold it. Made money. Next. After that, we bought a $997 course from DSG and followed it to turn the website building service into an enormous online course with perks included. Then we sold it. Made money.

But there was still a problem...

Every time that we wanted to make a change to our business model, we needed to buy another online course to see how that business model would run. The money we were spending on the courses was not the problem. The problem was that some were great, some were doozies, but many were outright scams. It was incredibly frustrating to not know what was about to happen whenever we clicked the "buy" button for a new course. We finally became fed up and decided to create a course reviewing system then buy courses and review them on YouTube. This way, others could see if a course was worth it or not. We chose to call it "Renae's Course Rating System." Clever, eh? I was out of ideas. We figured if we could create something that would make it possible to know if a course could truly help you make money from home legitimately, we would be really satisfied. After studying, creating and/or watching thousands of hours of courses and discovering what makes the courses legitimate or illegitimate, we created "Renae's Course Rating System." I can now know if a course is worth the value of the price tag and if that course will make you money if you follow it precisely. After we posted some course reviews on YouTube with "Renae's Course Rating System", we found that watchers really enjoyed the reviews as they could make a more informed decision on the courses that were right for them compared to the scams.

As a result of creating "Renae's Course Rating System" and buying courses based on a grade rating, I have been able to:

1. Buy valuable, legitimate courses that have helped me gain skills and knowledge.
2. Make over $5 million with the knowledge from those courses.
3. Help great course creators fund even more great courses.
4. Help hundreds of thousands of followers navigate through courses to help them make money according to the lifestyle that they want.

After creating "Renae's Course Rating System" to navigate through legitimate money-making courses, I was not only able to support my kids and husband in our million-dollar dream home, I have also been able to stop worrying about my kids being taken away from me or living in homeless shelters. We can now research and then grade an online course to see its legitimacy for whichever online business ladder we are ready to climb to make money.

All of this means that I have been able to recently have a fourth baby with my new husband, Tom Cote. Unlike the past, this time I am more than financially stable enough to care for our new baby and now all four of my children will be well taken care of. That was my goal. And now, the burden has been lifted from the days of being unable to pay those five dollars for my child's class party or any other items that I could not afford. Those days and that pain is over. But here is the thing…I am just like you but probably even dumber. I did not learn anything in school, received bad grades, and the other day I pronounced cognac as "kog-nack". The only difference between you and I is that

I found and took a few legitimate online courses and followed the necessary steps they instructed me to take. Legitimate online courses can help you no matter what online business model you want to run, no matter what industry you want to go into, and no matter what kind of money you want to make. There is an online course that can help you in your exact situation to get where you want to be, and it is the shortcut to get you there as fast as possible.

Don't believe me? More than forty percent of Fortune 500 companies regularly participate in online courses. **In 1995, only four percent of corporations used online courses. Now, ninety percent of corporations have shifted to learning from online courses.** Fortune 500 companies and corporations know that courses are the key to bringing in the bottom dollar at an unprecedented speed through legitimate shortcuts. If you really want to make money online without being scammed and do it all from home legitimately, courses are the way to go. Colleges do not want you to learn this invaluable lesson. They try to paint online courses as though they are not accredited and will only waste your time and money. But most of the time, college degrees are now a waste of time. I lived that dream. I wasted five years of my life getting my college degree and then quit to work from home. That college degree is not doing a damn thing for me now. At the same time though, you might be like me and feel afraid of being scammed by a weird coach guru who just takes your money and offers nothing in return. Or worse, they offer terrible advice that makes you lose even more money. Allow me to help you with this one.

How to tell if an online course is a scam within five minutes.

You might think, gee, online courses are online so the sellers might not be accountable or have real consequences. But the truth is, you can protect yourself with a single click before buying an online course. All the legitimate online courses have a terms and conditions page that you can click at the bottom of the sales page before purchasing the course. On this terms page, look for the words "returns," "refunds," or "cancelations." Read and take note of how many days you have to cancel your course purchase and if there are any strange loopholes such as needing to turn in homework. For me, each course I buy must have a no questions asked guarantee for at least 14 days, but 30 days is even better. No terms page at the bottom of the sales page? No refund guarantee within 14 or 30 days? Is homework required to get the refund? Please run far, far away. It is important to note that if you do buy the course, your credit card company should assist you with the refund if it is within 30 days. When I learned how easy it is to get in and out of bad courses if they had that refund guarantee on the terms page, I started buying courses left and right. Everything from email marketing, social media, sales copy, customer service strategies, and much more. I then built my business at lightning speed before any corporations or competitors could catch up. I started more businesses and used the updated course information each time to build those businesses too.

I now have a software company, a brick n mortar shop, an ecommerce company, and a keto cookbook company. I am now also helping my daughter build her online business the same way and with the same exact courses. Now, you might be thinking, ***I do not understand how a paid online course has information that a free YouTube video doesn't have. How is that possible?***

So, there was this dude named James Wedmore. I started my YouTube channel about one year after he started his. I became obsessed with his growth charts and comparing mine to his because I seemed to be consistently one year behind him so if I just kept going, I would be where he was the following year and so on. Then, suddenly, James Wedmore's YouTube growth charts shot through the moon, and I had no idea why. Did a video go viral? No. I was pulling out my hair trying to figure out what he did that I needed to achieve that same growth. I had watched every free YouTube video on YouTube growth, and it seemed as though I was doing everything exactly right. Then I saw something on his Instagram feed. I saw this blurred out white board behind him and he was sleeping on the couch. "What is THAT?!?" I thought, as I went crazy trying to figure out the blurred images on his white board. I watched even more free YouTube videos trying to find something similar. I lost sleep over it. A lot of sleep. I knew that this white board sketch was the key to his shooting up. Then, months later, after I completely forgot about it, I bought a new course. And in this new course, I saw a similar sketch. This was it. I precisely followed the sketch and voila! I shot up just like James Wedmore did. I do not know if it was the same course that James Wedmore bought, but it taught the same principles that I still, to this day, have not found for free on YouTube. Why haven't I been able to find it for free on YouTube? It is because the success is in the routine combination, not a single knowledge point. Let me explain.

If you were going to create your own swimming workout routine to challenge Michael Phelps in the Olympics, would you grab a bunch of free YouTube videos and put them together to try to win? Hell no…I would hope not! You need a winning training routine. Now, what if Michael Phelps' coach tells you that he will give you a copy of Michael Phelps' daily routine? This would give you access to the blueprint for everything he does from the moment he wakes up until the moment he goes to bed. Would you pay for that to challenge Michael Phelps, or would you say, "I'll just find something on YouTube"? The bottom line is that you are paying for an Olympic routine that works because of the step-by-step strategies in place from an expert. Now, some people think that all gurus are scammers because they may have started out making money one way, like ecommerce, but then they quit or sold their ecommerce business to sell a course on ecommerce. First, I do not know about you, but if I buy a course, I want someone who is in the teaching business full-time. If you quit your ecommerce business to teach me how to run my ecommerce business, I am not going to complain about it. I get more of your time and commitment. Yes, please! Also, do not judge because that is the ultimate American dream. To go make six figures and then teach others how to make six figures so you get to make seven figures teaching them how to do so. Then teach how to make seven figures and you make eight. You can do the same thing but first…learn how to make six figures online WITHOUT a course. Then make the course on how YOU made six figures.

Are you still not convinced?

If you were flipping burgers at McDonald's and you became good at it, then the manager offered you a raise to TEACH how to flip burgers perfectly, would you take it?

How To Get Your Money Back Instantly From Bad Online Courses Without Ruining Your Reputation

So, what if you feel as though you are not good at spotting the course scams because they all appear to be the same? Or maybe you are wondering how to know which ones offer the refunds within the guaranteed window. I totally hear you! Luckily for you, "Renae's Course Rating System" judges the course for you and gives you a grade so you know if you should refund or not. When I first started buying courses and trying them out, I had to follow them precisely to the end before finding out if they would work for me or not, or if I even enjoyed doing what the course wanted me to do. Some courses will make a lot of money, but do you want to kill yourself doing those things? There are so many ways of making money, you should enjoy the process. I would stay up all night watching and following the courses, and some would work, and others would not. I needed a faster way to judge if a course would work more by its sales page and by seeing some of the videos right away to know if the course were indeed a scam, outdated, or if it would actually work. I still remember taking this incredibly expensive $5,000 Amazon course back in 2016. I did not know at the time, but it was outdated. I watched this super extensive shipping section to get some planners that I had made in China shipped to the Amazon warehouse. To date, what happened for the following six months was some of the scariest, most stressful business moments I have ever gone through. I have never brought a Chinese product through freight forwarders, United States Customs, duties, or taxes. It involved palettes, logistics, several warehouses, boats, and 3,000 pounds of paperwork that I had no idea how to fill out. If I had filled the paperwork out incorrectly, my product would be sold off by the freight forwarder and lost forever. These people I was dealing with were all professionals. They did not like that I was a newbie asking them for help. They were rude and yelled at me for being what they deemed to be an idiot. I lost sleep. I cried. And I very rarely cry in business unless it is happy tears after a launch.

After the entire six-month headache, I took another Amazon course and learned that if I had just used the letters 'DDP' when dealing with the manufacturer, then they would have happily taken care of the entire process and I would have just waited for the planners to arrive at the Amazon warehouse. After this experience, I learned to always watch for up-to-date information in a course. If one thing is outdated, I bet the whole course is outdated. The strategy might even be outdated. REFUND! You might hear that story and think, "Wow, I just do not know if I could even learn a process like that." I am honestly not smart like that. I do not have a brain that works like that. But the truth is, if a course is made right, it is designed for dumb people.

No offense. I built a website building course called Architect. I designed it for tech-dumb people. I promise my students that, if you can send an email, you will have an ecommerce-based website by the time you are through with the course. I take my students through every single painstaking click from start to finish. I explain what some buttons mean and others I tell them they do not need to know what it means, just click it. And that is the way some of the most awesome courses are. They are like Mr. Miyagi in Karate Kid. Just paint the fence as instructed and then watch the money come out. Perhaps you don't have self-confidence. No problem. I would not be here if self-confidence were a requirement to make money online. You do not even have to believe that a course will work to follow it and see if it works.

When I bought that first $197 course, I didn't think it would work. It felt unnatural. I was skeptical. But I had tried my way for over a year and my way was not working. But before I gave up and took my kids to a homeless shelter, I thought I would at least give this course my all just so I could say I gave it my all before losing it all. So, when money started coming in after I tried the course, shock could not even begin to explain the feeling that I felt. You can be depressed, desperate, scared, sad and dumb…and still make money. As many ways as there are to make money online, there is an online course to shortcut you there. When I started a wedding invitation business online, it took me four years to hit the six-figure mark. That was before I realized that courses were not all scams and could help you make a lot more money than you think. Fast forward to when I had my YouTube channel, after I took that first paid course, it took me three years to hit seven-figures. What a difference a course or so could make.

Still not convinced that online courses are the way to go? The online course industry is expected to surpass $243 billion in 2022. More and more people are realizing that they can skip the college electives and dive right into a specialty and start making money right away. And the more specialized you choose to become, the more money you can make. Example: A lot of people want to be photographers yet very few realize that Amazon company's look for Amazon specialized photographers and will pay 10x's more for someone who knows the specialized skill. Learn the skill from an online course in Amazon photography. Practice, get it exactly right and BOOM! Money.

You might be thinking '*what if I waste my time and money and change my mind later?*' It took me five years and $60,000 to get my communications degree in college then six months working at a newspaper after graduation to realize, I do not want to work as an editor at a paper, I want to work from home and run an online business. The good news about online courses is that you can spend a lot less and try the actual field you are going to work in to see if you like it without spending anything close to $60,000 or waiting five years to make it happen. I have tried many businesses that I only failed because I quit. But that was because I did not enjoy the work. I started writing a blog and I thought I would be doing that for 20 years. Then I turned on a camera, fell in love with YouTubing and decided I no longer liked writing the blog. It will be the same for you. Be willing to adapt to your feelings so you land where you are willing to work. You will not know exactly what that will be right away. So be ok with trying several different business models until you find something that you do not mind the grind work of. You will need to pay your dues just like you would in any other industry. But do the work and hone your craft and you will easily be able to make money from home.

But wait…you are probably thinking, "*How do I know which online course to buy?*" Allow me to help you with this one as well.

CHAPTER 3

Fevers and Poison

To know which course and coach that you need, you must catch a fever and then taste your own brand of poison. Let me explain. Have you ever been told that you work too hard and need to relax? That is the story of my life. It's a bad habit. I know. It's like a dark drug addiction.

I cannot stop working. I am obsessed with winning the next level of the business video game. I call that an EntreGamer. Because of this, I have no friends, except those who do not tell me to relax. My only friends these days are people who never use phrases like "Slow down", or "You're working too hard", or "You never spend time with us anymore." Once someone says that I work too hard and that it threatens our friendship, that friendship is over. You just threatened our relationship by saying that and now we are doomed forever. Goodbye! Sorry, not sorry.

Isn't that how all addictions take over though? I am not saying that it's right. I am saying that it's why I cannot even stop to patch up strained relationships. Why do I do it? Why do I work like this just for the next hit of euphoria, which may or may not come at all? When I get in this mode, I just feel as though nothing exists outside of the work, and I am plugged in until I die, which I call a fever. Others call it things like commitment, drive, dedication, or ambition. You know, other words that sound a bit more honorable. But the truth is, for us entrepreneurs where business runs in our blood, it is more like a fever. *Just get out of the way so I can get things accomplished.* The phrase I often use is, "I'm sorry. I just have to do this." And then I come up for air about four months later. My husband Tom calls me a kite that he must constantly keep out of the trees. No, he does not try to tame me. But he does keep me tethered to the ground just enough to eat, sleep, and say hello to the kids as he watches for trees that I may not see. Tom Cote will always be the love of my life because when I get a fever, he understands it. He steps up in other areas that enable me to work harder, and then he tells me sweet things like "I'll miss you, but I'll see you on the other side of that fever." Then, when I am done, I buy him big ole gifts such as a $28,000 side by side to snow plow the driveway. However, sometimes I get in way over my head, and I come out apologizing because… welp…I just lost us a ton of money and now I must go into a second four-month fever to get us out of the mess. I guess that is what happens when you are reckless. You get reckless rewards, but you also get reckless losses that you need to fix quickly.

Is my work-a-holic-ness wrong? Yes. Of course, it is. Will I stop? No, I cannot. I am addicted and will play if I have that fever. Can I control the fever? Could I relax if I really wanted to? No. I cannot control when the fever hits or ends. For example, I could go to the beach on a beautiful day and all I will be thinking about is when we are going to go home so I can get back to work. I cannot stop the fever while it is going. There is not a drug on this planet that can tame it either. A fever typically hits right before I start a major project and it always ends as I'm about to complete it. Sometimes I will think about a project and wish I had a fever for it, but the fever never comes. Other times, I get a fever for something dumb, and I try to argue with the fever. It does not work. The fever always wins, and I must follow through with the work until the fever ends. I never have enough fever to get me through an entire project. The fever abandons me, and I get angry with it. Sometimes, I will talk to the fever. "Where did you go?" or, "We aren't done yet...Don't abandon me now!" Although, do not worry, I am aware of who is really answering back. I go on to finish the big project that the fever started and then completely abandoned me with. I should just abandon the project, right? Nope. Cannot. If I abandon the project when my fever goes away it means that I will not get the next fever. And as much as I hate the fever when it abandons me or gets me into trouble, I cannot live without it. I must finish and that will earn me my next fever. I live for that next fever when the current one runs out...just like a drug.

Most normal people do not understand what a fever is. They mistake it for stress or anxiety. They see it as something that should be controlled. But it does not work that way. Stress and anxiety are what you feel. I feel a fever. I need another hit. Success for me revolves around this fever. I do not choose the fever; the fever chooses me. Sometimes we win, sometimes we lose. But I will chase that next fever the same way I did my previous one. Now, this fever is addicted to poison. And not just any poison, my fevers get addicted to a specific brand of poison. I will not ever know what that brand of poison is until I try it for thirty days and see if my fever likes the poison. I know, I am sick, just go with it for now. When I tried YouTube, I expected to hate it. After thirty days, I could not stay away from the poison. But most people who try YouTubing quit after ten videos or less. Why? They thought they would be spending ten minutes recording themselves, uploading and reading comments from fans all day and laughing all the way to the bank. No, my friend. You spend two hours planning, fifteen minutes recording, six hours editing, and then eight hours marketing and building out your business infrastructure. And when you finally get to the comments? It is a total weirdo that heard you say, "this business thing is hard" and they say creepy things like "I'm coming for you and my bride will wear white." What the hell does that mean? OMG, I am getting murdered tonight. Now THAT is a weird poison to love, no?

A lot of people say to shadow different careers before you go to college to see if you will really like it. Well, there are different online business models that all have a different poison. You should try them before committing. And if you catch a fever during one of them, you will not be able to leave that business model even if you logically try to tell your head why you *should* leave. That is when you will succeed. That is what you are meant to do. That is the coach and course you will want to find.

At the beginning of the 2020 global pandemic, I had a lot of fans that suddenly had businesses in trouble. "What do we do Renae?" they asked me via email. Welp…we must try to find an easy way for them to make money online while they are building their other businesses. I did not expect what would happen next. I started testing different business models on YouTube in front of the world to see. Nothing was off the table, not even what normal people would consider scams. An app where you fill out surveys and it makes money? Let's try it! Here is why I did not ever dismiss anything, even get rich quick schemes. Every business model can be explained away as to why it will not work. Just like every diet can. *"Oh, that business will not work because it is against that platform's terms of service. Oh, that business will not work because of this giant competitor. Oh, that business will not work because it is saturated. Oh, that business will not work because it requires this one skill set."* I didn't listen. I didn't care. Why? Because the ways I found to make money in the past are all ways people told me were not possible. So, I do not listen to experts, college professors, textbooks, people who have written 'habits' books, the average man or woman, and especially not my own fans. No offense fans. You are almost always wrong. Everyone's reasons for why it will not work are excuses to me until I try it. Because…fevers and poisons. What if I find something that a fan gets a fever over, they try it, and they find it is their brand of poison? Now that I am testing different business models live and passing them onto others with fevers, I am not just into entregamer drugs. I am now the entregamer drug dealer. "Here, let me show you what it's like and you can decide if you want to try it!" Bottom line, there is always a way to make anything work if it is your brand of poison that you want. So, I set out to test brands of poison for my audience. What happened next shook me and my own belief systems about business. I thought tests on Etsy would work and they did not. I thought tests on eBay with drop shipping would not work and they did. I thought tests on Amazon would fail and they worked. And I thought tests on Pinterest would work and they failed. Does that mean that Etsy and Pinterest do not work? They work. But it means you must really enjoy their poison to win on those platforms. If you are that person that wants easier money and you do not mind "monotony poison", then eBay drop shipping will work for you. This is because all eBay drop shipping is, is listing Walmart products on eBay to sell repeatedly all day long. Boring as hell, but I am still making money with it, and I have an assistant running it who does not mind monotony poison. I would kill myself if it were me. I cannot take that kind of poison.

If you are a person that does not want to get creative or make your own products, but you want to sell other company's products on Amazon, then you can contact brands and become their Amazon agent and make a ton of money. But...You must not mind "extrovert poison" because each day, all day long you are on the phone attempting to convince brands to let you be their agent. Yes, you can make millions with this. But I do not do it. Not my poison. If you are that person who wants to build your own trademarked product brand, and get in front of a gazillion eyes, and you do not mind "dictator poison", then Amazon is for you. Yes, you can make millions. But it is more expensive than any other business model and riskier as well. Now THIS is my type of poison. I do not know why, but my fever chooses this. I am not allowed to ask it questions. I just follow it where it goes. Sometimes it gets me into trouble. But I always find a way out. This is my poison.

So, you want to grow a handmade business on Etsy and work until your fingers fall off. All of that just to hear one more person ask you for a 75% discount code or the pattern for what you made so they do not have to pay you? If this is you then you must not mind "unappreciated poison." The reason is you will not make a lot of money on Etsy, very few do. The statistics are staggering. But the ones who do make it, do not mind making a dollar an hour by the time they are finished making a product. A lot of my followers have this poison. I must be honest…I do not understand it at all. But I support it. Wait…you DO want to do YouTube videos even though you heard how time consuming it is to get out a three-minute video? Then you must not mind "masochistic poison". Because whatever you imagine the YouTuber lifestyle to be…it is not that. It is not glamorous. No one in real life or online respects you. Your friends laugh at you and treat you like you are a clown. You are not allowed to have a single bad day, or your reputation is ruined for life. And if you do not serve your audience 365 days a year, then your audience will consider you a selfish jerk. They will tell you that you are only looking out for yourself. Oh! And then you also must make sure you get some kick ass security because you will get threats. Does this sound fun? Then your fever might be calling out for this masochistic poison.

Back to my drug dealing business model tests live on YouTube. This is how it worked in real time for everyone to see. I would lay a test out to my audience in a short video and ask the audience to bet if I would succeed or fail. I received a total mix of opinions from me being a total idiot who knows nothing to me being a brilliant genius who just came up with the next million-dollar idea. I would not listen to any of it. Instead, I would test it and track it and report on the results of what happened. Then I would get a whole different slew of opinions. If the test failed, I would be blamed because I did not choose to do the test a different way, even though just as many people bet my test would work. Usually, those comments would be from some smart ass and start with the phrase "This is why…" and then they go onto some college grad analysis of how to run a business. What is it they call that? A Monday morning quarterback? They would spout their knowledge as if there is no way a business could fail if they follow their college textbook. As if starting and running a business is not a risk at all if you follow that textbook. Whatever. "Just find your fever and your poison," I would say. And if you are reading this, you should do the same. Start researching different ways of making money online. You can start with my channel to see how it works. Then, if you do not mind the poison and you catch a fever…well …there is nothing more to say in that case. You will succeed. The fever will not let you fail if you finish. Get to know yourself, get that fever, and you will not mind the poison. Now, this is important because some of the ways to make money online are more complicated. Yes, you can try yourself, watch free YouTube videos and dive in to see if it is for you. But you should absolutely find a course to go with your business model if you catch a fever for it. A course can be the shortcut to winning faster in that business model. If the course has that money back guarantee, usually between 14 days to 30 days, then you should be able to get a taste of the coach and course to see if it fits with your fever and poison. If it does not? Then do not be afraid to refund and move onto the next course. I have wasted a lot of money on courses but the ones that made me millions more than made up for all the bad ones. It does help now that I have "Renae's Course Rating System" to know if a course should be kept or tossed.

Would you like "Renae's Course Rating System" for yourself to help you with your own journey? Alright then...

Granted!

CHAPTER 4

Renae's Course Rating System

Renae's Course Rating System has ten elements that make up an entire grade. Each element is graded out of 10 as well. This way, after the ten elements are graded 10/10, we can get a proper percentage as well as a letter grade, A, B, C, D, F. This has not prevented me from purchasing scams or bad courses. But it sure helps me to know if I should ask for my money back right away if I get in there and see some red flags.

These elements will also help you to know if the course will work or if it is just fluff and of little substance. And if you are going for a money-making course, these elements are even more important. When I see them in a money-making course, and they receive a great grade, I know the worst-case scenario is that by the time I am through, I will make money. Period. The only question left is how much. Now, obviously this does not 100% guarantee that you will make money from a money-making course if the grade is high. Other variables exist such as your own level of understanding, the amount and speed that you execute, and most of all, your adaptability if, or when, something goes wrong. Also, this rating system does not include market variables of what you are going into. For example, if you love that Etsy poison of working full-time for almost nothing, you will make less than someone who chooses Amazon. There is an Etsy course that shows you how to make money and an Amazon course that shows you how to make money. But because of market stats, you will most likely make more on Amazon. So, consider that when you get your fever, and you do the research on the platforms that you tie yourself to. Think and research industry statistics before diving into a course as well to help you with this.

Element #1: Money Back Guarantee (no homework)

I never ever recommend someone buy a course without a money back guarantee. Ever. In fact, if we get to this point, and there is no guarantee, I will not finish the grading system. You get an automatic F and I have moved onto something else. I always offer a money back guarantee for my courses and I only support those that do as well. Why? Because people can only digest the sales page so much before they click 'buy' and once they get in, what if it wasn't what they thought it was? What if they made some assumptions based on the sales page to only find out that they were dead wrong and now the course is not for them? What if they get inside and you say "Bestie" every other word and it annoys the hell out of them. They might want out. It is so greedy if you cannot offer a money back guarantee. Think about those who could only hear so much of what you were selling them while you throw a timer in front of their face this way they must rush to get in or they won't get another shot, so they do so and now they get in and realize…snap…I just made a big mistake. You are going to pressure them like that, get them to purchase emotionally and then not let them out at that point? What are you? Hotel California? Give me a break. Quit. Do not be a coach. Only scammers do that because it is the only way they can keep their money. Your stuff is garbage if you must do that. Leave. Go flip a burger. Can you tell I feel strongly about this? I do not have the same fired up emotions about the other 9 elements, but I want to be extremely clear that you should look for that money-back guarantee on the sales page and click through to the terms page to make sure there are no weird strings attached. Some courses offer a money-back guarantee for small things like, if you give them a full explanation of why you want the feedback so they can better their course. Fine! Other courses offer a money-back guarantee for bigger things that trap you like…you must do ALL the homework from module 1 and do it correctly. Imagine sixty somersaults and if you do one somersault wrong then no, no refund. So, if you see the money-back guarantee badge on the sales page, then that is cool. But click through on the terms page to make sure there are not heavy strings attached to that.

Element #2: Shortcut

This element is opposite of what most people value courses with. Most people, when they want to buy a course they ask, "Well how much is in there? How many hours of video? How big is it?"

They do this because they equate length with value, when really, they should be equating short with value. I could sell a course with 1,000 hours of video containing a strange dude reading the alphabet repeatedly. Or I could sell a 1-hour course showing you how I made my first million as I take you through each step and give you all my shortcuts. Maybe I even give you my little black book of contacts and suppliers. That is worth far more than the number of hours. In fact, when I hear the number of hours in a course, when the hours seem extensive compared to the topic, they get a lower grade on this element. The reason we are purchasing the course and spending money on it is because your course is supposed to be the private jet to my destination. I do not want to take the car across the country, give me the jet. I recently watched a course that had jammed each video so tightly that I had to watch each one three times while writing like wildfire to keep up. That is the course I want! Give me the shortcut to the money. I want it like Einstein. Einstein said, "everything in life should be as simple as possible but not simpler."

Do not bloat the course with unnecessary drivel. Hashtag #DontBloatTheCourse. Now, in comparison to college, college would receive an extremely bad grade. College makes you learn a lot of extras that have nothing to do with your career. I got my degree in communications, and I was forced to take a course on Women's Studies where we talked about how men always get to have careers while the women stay home with their baby. *WHY ARE YOU MAKING ME TAKE THIS*?!? This is one reason I am such a fan of online courses now instead of college. I did that. I got my bachelor's degree. It's totally useless. The first $197 course

I bought led me to millions and was two hours long. Now that's value. That is the shortcut I want.

Element #3: Binge Capability (or drip-fed)

The next element of Renae's Course Rating System is more of a personal preference but with reasoning behind it. First, I am a total Netflix binger and I soak up information like a sponge. Do not lock the next module of the course because you are concerned about my level of overwhelm. I am an adult. Let me handle my own overwhelm. If you have never had this happen, let me explain. You purchase an online course and pretend it has 12 modules. That is kind of like chapters or sections but in courses we call them modules. So, you go to the first module and watch the videos and you are now ready for the second module but…oops…locked. You must wait until X date or after X days to watch it. WHYYYYYYYYYYYY?!? According to the course creators who do this, they are trying to "help you" so you do not get overwhelmed. Stop it. We are not 8 years old. People who cannot handle their overwhelm should not be in your course and they should not be trying to make money online. The truth is most course creators do this because they want to keep their best stuff locked up until after the money-back guarantee expires. So, you can have a taste of module 1 and see if it is right for you but you will get module 2 after the thirty-day guarantee is over. Every course has a different drip-fed system and guarantee so they are not all like that. But, if you get in and it is a drip-fed course, pay attention to the information you get before the guarantee day. What if that information alone is not enough to keep the course? Get out and get your refund. It is not worth it and there are plenty of other courses that give you the entire course with your payment so you can Netflix binge.

Now, some people disagree with me on this. They like drip-fed courses. Maybe it feels more like college. They have time to go get their little notebook with stickers, stamps, and planners. So, if that is you, I will not judge you if you will not judge me for wanting to binge the course like a fat kid with a chocolate cake. Speaking of chocolate cake, my husband Tom has the recipe for the best chocolate cake I have ever had in my life! Want the recipe? Okay!

Wait…this is a business book; we can't put a chocolate cake recipe in a business book!

Do not ask questions, just make the cake!

The Best Chocolate Cake Ever

- 1 box devil's food cake mix
- 1 small pkg Jello instant chocolate pudding mix
- 1 cup sour cream
- 1 cup vegetable oil
- 4 eggs, beaten
- ½ cup milk
- 1 tsp vanilla
- 2 cups mini chocolate chips

Preheat the oven to 350 degrees F. In a large bowl, mix everything except the chocolate chips. Batter will be thick. Stir in the chocolate chips. Pour batter into the cake pan of choice (I normally use two 9-inch pie pans). For cooking time, I use the cooking times on the back of the devil's food cake box as a guide and usually add 10 minutes to whatever it says. Then I do the toothpick check and if it is not done, I check on it every five minutes after that. It usually takes around 45 minutes for two, 9-inch pie pans.

Buttercream Frosting

- 1 cup shortening (Crisco)
- 4 cups powdered sugar
- 1/4 tsp salt
- 1 tsp vanilla extract
- 1/3 cup heavy whipping cream

In a mixing bowl, cream shortening until fluffy. Add sugar and continue creaming until well blended. Add salt, vanilla, and whipping cream. Blend on low speed until moistened. Beat at high speed until the frosting is fluffy.

Element #4: Step by Step

This element is one of the most critical for success and so many courses do not have it. To me, a course is an educational documentary without this element. For a course to be worth its cost, the instructor must show me, step by step, how to get a result at the end of their instructions without any skipped or missing instructions. For example, if I am selling a course to a five-year-old on how to tie his/her shoes, I am going to tell them how to get those shoes tied and at the end? They better have their shoes tied. Some courses show more of 'what' you need to do and 'why', but they do not show you the 'how'. This is important because if you do not show how then no one will get a result at the end. Now when I say this, I do not mean busy work. For example, some courses, when talking about your target market, give you a worksheet and say, "describe your perfect customer" or "describe your target market" or "describe your avatar." All three of these things mean the same thing. Listen to me, who the hell cares? If I wish for the perfect customer, they are not coming through the door. In fact, most of the businesses that I have built ended up attracting a different target market than I originally intended. If you cannot say it in a phrase, "I'm selling ______ to _______" then you are going too far until you know who your product will attract. It is then easy because you are gathering that data instead of making it up. I am selling 'Keto Cookbooks' to 'Keto Dieters'. Is that so hard? Come on! We don't need a whole module on that, and we don't need a worksheet to go with it.

Also, most of the time when coaches ask you to do that exercise, they can never offer concrete help beyond having you and him/her as a coach making something up in your head that you do not really know will come to fruition. I am not saying the target market isn't important. I am saying, launching a product to an audience and then gathering data is better than making up your target market from the beginning. Now, you might be thinking, 'how do we know if what the coach is giving us is busy work or if it is important, right? Because you must follow your course precisely before you know if it reaps rewards and results, right?' Well…that is just the thing. You might go through more than one course before you realize what works and what does not. Fluff versus substance. But one thing that always gives me a huge hint is the next element.

Element #5: Olympic Routine(s)

This is the biggest element that will tell me if I'll make money from a money-making course or not. This one, no one else talks about and, in fact, most people value the opposite of this. Let me explain. You know those Dummy Books? Build a Business for Dummies? eBay for Dummies? That sort of thing? Those types of books and courses give all the options. You can do path A, path B, path C all the way to path Z. One expert's theory is this while another is that. It is like an encyclopedia of a topic instead of you learning about what you need to do and what brings in the most money. Worthless. So let me ask you a question. If you had to compete against 23-time gold medalist, Michael Phelps, in the Olympics next year, would you read a 'Swimming for Dummies' book? Would you piece together your own workout routine from all the free videos on YouTube? Or would you get a coach? And why would you get a coach? What could that coach really offer that the 'Dummies' book or free YouTube videos do not?

I will tell you. It is an Olympic routine.

Remember, what if Michael Phelps' coach offered to give you every second of every day of Michael Phelps' physical routine from the moment he woke up to the moment he went to sleep? What if the coach also offered you his nutrition routine, everything he eats from the morning when he wakes up to the moment he goes to bed? What if he gives you Michael Phelps' competition routine? What does Michael do on competition days from the moment he wakes up to the moment he gets to the event center to the moment he gets in the pool and pushes off? What if he tells you everything Michael Phelps' thinks every day and on competition days and what Michael Phelps' focuses on when things get hard? Now, obviously if you took his same everything and competed against him, he still might slay you. But how much closer would you be than if you tried free YouTube videos or a 'Dummies' book with all the options? You see, I do not want the options. I want the Olympic routine of the coach. If the coach made a million dollars in a specific way, I want that routine. Give it to me! Then, even if I do not make a million, I am still going to be closer than following free YouTube videos. Which, I have proven by the way. I have made way more money when I have bought courses that are Olympic routines and I have lost more money by following free YouTube videos. So, does this suddenly mean that all the coaches with the Lamborghinis might be legitimate?!? OMG Yes actually! Well, maybe. If they have a money-back guarantee, I will then get in and check out their Olympic routine next. Are they really selling what they did themselves? Or is it a plethora of different ways, methods, and theories? I want one way, your way, and I want the shortcut. Too demanding? Ha! There is more that I want.

Element #6: Complete

Obviously, a course cannot cover every topic under the sun, but it should cover everything needed to get the result at the end of your course. For example, if that five-year-old needs a specific shoe to tie a knot a certain way, you better be giving me a short-cut link to that shoe so I can succeed. Or, maybe an even better example, if your whole course sells me on the idea of becoming an Amazon Sales Agent for wholesale products, and in the course you give me a copy and paste email to send to brands that say things like, "I am a wiz at Amazon PPC ads", then you better damn well teach me to be a wiz at Amazon PPC ads so that I know how to run the business model you're touting. This was a major problem in a recent Amazon course that I reviewed on my channel. The course was a few thousand dollars, and it was about selling myself to brands to get deals. However, there were just a few bonus videos afterwards that did not teach me how to be a good Amazon Agent and perform well with the tasks I was promising that I could do for these brands. I could sell a solar system to my neighbor, promise to install it, get the money but when it comes time to install it? Now what do I do?! That is what this awful course felt like.

Usually, the completion of what you need with the course is found in course bonuses. If a course is about Etsy, you should be teaching Etsy SEO to get your listing ranked. If your course is on Facebook ads, you better show how to get Facebook tracking installed as well as the FB Pixel Helper Chrome Extension to make sure it was installed correctly.

Element #7: Hand Holding

This one is for newbies.

Many courses teach and they start from an intermediate or advanced phase of what they are teaching. I know it is difficult as a coach to go back to the very beginning of when you first heard about the subject you are teaching about, so this is a rare skill that a teacher must hone. It also shows a seasoned course and a good instructor because newbies will ask newbie questions and a good instructor will pay attention to those and put that information into the course, even after they have created the course. The instructor will add it as an update later. I have also seen some instructors make an entire wiki directory that can be searched for things like this as well. But knowing newbie questions is not the only aspect that goes into the hand-holding element.

Hand Holding means that the instructor basically takes you by the hand to go through each step of their course. Do they have to do that? Nope. Do they have to have other support teams do that? Nope. It just means that the course itself does that. For example, I made a course showing how to build a website from scratch. My ultimate promise was that, if you can send an email, you can build a website with my course. Now, this is a bold promise and I found that out as people started flooding my course. I had to make videos in between other videos to show newbies how to copy and paste and unzip a folder to their computer desktop. But, at the end of the day, if someone follows me click by click, then they are hand-held through to finishing a website. The major aspect of the hand holding element is showing 'how' to do something instead of 'what' or 'why' via hand holding guidance. If you are telling me that I need a specific software to succeed, show me click by click how to use that software. Show me how you have the software set up. Show me what to click in the software to become successful. What is important in that software? What should I NEVER touch?

That is hand holding.

Element #8: Updates

This grade can differ depending on if a course is evergreen or not. What is evergreen? To the online business world when you say 'evergreen' it simply means timeless. Evergreen cannot ever become dated. Some business principles have been used from the beginning of time and will work 3,000 years from now. That is evergreen. Once taught, you do not need to continually update that content in your course unless you show your face, and you are suddenly ten years younger than your sales video. Then you should probably update it. Most courses try to use as much evergreen teaching as possible. This makes it easy to sit back and basically retire as all you must do is funnel ads to your course. Then people are delivered their product, and you are pretty much done for the rest of your life. Evergreen courses can be just as valuable as courses that need to be updated due to technology changing, but people tend to buy the technology updated courses more. For example, in my website building course, I use twenty different software and website builders and plugins to help you build it. All of them are either free or I paid for the license for you to have it free with the course. But it takes a full-time staff to keep that course updated because almost every single day, one of those software or plugins change its interface and no one knows where to click. I once paid someone $10,000 to redo the training completely from scratch. And within 24 hours of them finishing and handing it over to me, the main software we used did a major update and the entire thing had to be done over again. Why do I do it? I am sick. Do not ask why. Also, you need a website. So... just do not ask why. The more a course is updated, the better the course instructor and the more power they have of delivering a superb product to their students. Updates are more than just updates. Updates mean that the course has made enough students money and that the coach and course is being recommended to others. They are becoming successful by recommending others and the coach is raking in enough money to continually update their course through themselves or a staff. Updates show the quality of the course, the stamina of the coach, and the power behind the company. Think about it. Most course purchases come with updates for life. What value is that if they never update it again? So, you want to pay attention to the coach with the Lamborghini more than the others because he is the one that will be around to update the course. And if his or her students have Lamborghinis, then that coach probably has several staff members doing all sorts of things to make things easier for you.

One Amazon coach that I have worked with had such successful students that he was able to build out multiple staffs here in the states and in China so he could deliver products and sourced manufacturers on a silver platter. He had seven layers of support for his students. I have never seen another coach be able to do that before. And once I bought his course, I understood how he could do that. I was about to make a lot of money and recommend him. And he will use that money to add on even more.

Element #9: Support

We have just spoken a lot about support and that is our next element. One mistake I have seen most people make is that they value a course only when they can talk to the instructor personally or ask questions directly to the instructor in the Facebook group. This is cool but the truth is, if that instructor's course is so tight, and full of handholding, you will not need to talk to the instructor. Period. I have tried to make my courses that way. If I see a specific question being asked repeatedly in one of my groups, I will make a video with that question and its answer right in the course. This way, it not only saves company resources, but it makes my course even more of a shortcut. You do not even have to go get support. It is all in the course! Having said that, most courses offer support if someone makes their own assumptions, or they feel like they are a special exception to the course steps. What do I do if I am in this unique situation? Right? And you do not know if that will be you. That could be a legitimate thing. I was trying to sell products on Amazon, and I had a backlog of products from a baby shop. Do I put them up on Amazon or am I wasting my time? Should I first focus on the main product in the course? How many other people have a backlog of products from a baby shop? Um…no one. I got an answer in the Facebook group within a few minutes. They pretty much said, "might as well" which to me means 'worst case scenario, we make money'.

Support is important and it is valuable in case you get stuck. But do not use it as a crutch. The real value of the course is in the Olympic Routine and the step-by-step shortcut. The support is only partially valuable compared to those things. I would pay ten times more to buy a course with a wicked, handheld, step by step, shortcut driven, Olympic routine than something lengthy college textbook options and a ton of 1-on-1 meetings or support. But still, consider support depending on your situation and grade accordingly.

Element #10: Value

Ah, yes. The final element for Renae's Course Rating System. This element and grade, surprisingly enough, is subjective. This one is harder to grade when you have not bought a lot of courses. I have this element in my rating system because I have purchased dozens of courses and can compare them all with one another in value. When grading this element, I ask myself the question, "How much would I pay for this course if I had to pay again?" Would I pay the same amount that I paid after I have gone through it completely and watched everything inside? Did it hold up to my other elements after going through the entire thing? Would I pay less? Would I pay more?

It is rare that I find a course that I feel has charged the accurate price. I always feel they should have charged less and there was not enough step by step help, it was incomplete, or I felt they should have charged more, sometimes even ten times more. I give them a standing ovation in my home with my kids and husband watching me like I just landed from outer space. You will be able to grade this after you buy a few courses yourself and you will quickly know if a course is worth the cost after some experience. Do not be afraid to lose money though. Remember, we do not even look at a course if it does not have that money-back guarantee!

Just make sure you time it to get out before that guarantee expires if you need to. Wait...do some coaches give that guarantee and not honor it? In short, they would not be in business for long. It is too easy to start an 'I hate _____' Facebook page for the world to see that the instructor does not accept the guarantee that they tout. Also...your credit card company will side with you if you show them the terms and sales pages. Refund. Cancel. Bye! Now, what do you do once you find a coach and course that you are ready to follow with precision?

Let me give you some advice for what you do not realize is coming down the pike.

CHAPTER 5

Let The EntreGames Begin

After you have dabbled enough to catch a fever, tasted your own brand of poison, and picked a course and an instructor, then you are ready to start your EntreGame. You, my friend, are the EntreGamer. Think of it like playing a video game. This does not have to be painful beyond tasting your brand of poison.

I realize that a lot of 'habits' and 'millionaire success' books talk about the right mindset to have. But here is everything I know after fifteen years of success and hobnobbing with the authors of those books...They are all lying. If they can convince you that mindset is so important and if you fail, it is because you have the wrong mindset, then they have an excuse for their training to stink. The truth is, I never had that 'be tough or die' mindset and neither did anyone else that I know who has succeeded in business. In fact, when I first started trying different business models, I had more of a Dumb and Dumber reaction to it. If you have never seen Dumb and Dumber, I do not recommend wasting your time on it. But in the movie, Jim Carrey (loser) is chasing Mary Swanson (hot chick). He finally gets up the courage to ask her about his odds with her. "The least you can do is level with me. What are my **chances**?" He asks. Her response? "Not good." He persists. "You mean, not good like one out of a hundred?" She answers, "I'd say more like one in a million." Jim Carrey then delivers one of the most epic lines of the movie, "So you're telling me there's a chance."

I too saw the statistic that 9 out of 10 businesses fail. All I thought was, "Okay, so I have to start 10 businesses and one of them will succeed. Sweet!" Ironically, it really did take about ten for one to finally succeed at a breadwinning level. Now, every time I start a new EntreGame I say the same thing to my husband, "Would it be ridiculous if I can actually do this? How ridiculous would this be?" This is what I said at the grand opening of my brick n mortar baby shop. I continued, "All you need to know about me is that I'm a YouTuber and no one should be letting me do this!" I turned to Tom later that day and said "It's so ridiculous that the town let me do that. I totally thought they would stop me." Meet the new you. This is your new mindset.

"So, you're saying there's a chance" and "Would it be ridiculous if I won this EntreGame?"

Play the video game ten times as an entregamer and one time you will probably win. How many times have you played video games and died ten times before winning and beating the entire game? I am not sure about you but when I played Super Mario, I would die ten times in one level, not just the whole game, and I kept playing. It was always those stupid fish levels too. I hate the water levels. They suck! Anyway, most successful entrepreneurs are more like entregamers. When they lose, they do not sit in pity and say, "Will anything ever go right? I need to meditate for three years, and I don't even know if I'll ever try again because maybe it doesn't work. Maybe it's not for me." Who has this mindset when playing a video game? No one, or else you are a total loser.

Now, obviously you do not want to keep trying at something that truly will not work, like beating your head on a brick wall. I have news for you, that brick wall is forever. Your head, not so much if you keep beating it against the brick wall. But that is what the business models and courses and industry research is for. The rest is a video game, and you keep playing and trying different techniques to win. Hmmmm...Maybe a particular ad does not work. I wasted video game credits on it. Do I quit? Or do I try a new ad? Do I sit and say, "ads don't work, clearly, I tried that!" or do you try again? What would you do in the video game? I am actually saddened by all the mindset talk about 'wanting to succeed bad enough that you want to breathe'. That is a terrible mindset because the entregamer in the Mario Kart dune buggy just flew past your little...mindset adventure. Being video game competitive prevails over a 'must do this" mindset any day of the week.

Don't believe me?

Smell anyone in a normal business convention and smell someone after they have been playing video games for three days straight without taking a break. That is how addicted they are. They play and play and play some more. They are addicted and no one can stop them except maybe their mom to make them take out the garbage. And the only reason they do that is because their mom will fuel them with enough chips to last on their video game another day. I know this is what gamers do…I dated several in high school! Their favorite poison was Final Fantasy IIV. Mine? I was running the newspaper in high school. My first business. That was my video game, and I was just as addicted. I have a hard time understanding anyone with a 'suffer for your business' type of discipline. Of course, it is work. I am not saying that it's not. Video games also take a ton of work to win. But when I started YouTube in 2012, I taught basic business principles that I used to succeed so others could do the same and succeed as well. I could not find anyone else teaching women basic business principles at that time. Everyone teaching women was teaching topics like 'work life balance' and 'how to save and set a budget'. *What the heck?* I thought when I saw these. *Women need what the men have but they probably won't listen to men with their Lamborghini's, so I'll teach them*, I thought.

Things caught on quickly and people were seeing results right away. I prided myself on doing zero motivational videos because I considered them fluff. We have work to do. What a waste of time! But I quickly learned that some people suffer and need the motivation to act. I had one friend who became a client. Because she had my direct texting number, she thought that means she gets all access to me, any time, day or night. The situation became complicated quickly because, if this person's business failed, it could result in our relationship deteriorating as well. I loved this friend, so I was bound and determined to make this person's business wildly successful. It was the strangest business I ever tried to build. Not because she had a bad product; she had one of the best products I had seen on the market. It was strange because she would throw temper tantrums at me at least once a month. My friend was ultimately miserable every day and was determined to complain and let me know it about once every month. I would try to explain what she needed to do and send her videos and she would pout and say "I'm quitting" until I showed up at her house and did it for her. I built her entire website, added her products, and clicked to go live and she had a meltdown. A complete panic attack and begged me to turn the site off because she was not ready. I taught her how to build and launch product lines and she would build them, get them ready, post them to her website, then take them down immediately. She would say that she needed to redo the whole thing because it was not what she imagined. I was trying different ways of talking to her because, again, my friend's relationship with me was important. I was willing to try anything to help this person succeed, even to the point that I did everything for her. At one point I thought maybe I needed a repertoire of motivational sayings that I could just text her when she felt that way. That did not work. It made her angrier and she would yell at me in text. I kept thinking, "wow that really hurts…she can't be trying to hurt me on purpose. She must not realize how hurtful she is being. I am doing everything for her that I have never done for anyone else!" And then the next month would come and the same hatred would be sent my way via text message. This went on every month for three years. One time I thought that maybe she just wanted me to give her an out and I'll just tell her it's not a big deal if she wants to do something else? Nope. That ticked her off more than anything.

I noticed something during those three years though. She was not doing a lot of work. Oh, she was creating a lot of products, but they sat in her kitchen and never went up on the website to be sold. If I mentioned this, she yelled "I'm doing a LOT of work! I work all the time!" However, I noticed that this person kept a perfect house, perfect pets, perfect kids, and perfect meals for her husband and stayed in great shape. I hate to say it...but she had a different video game. None of that would be perfect if she were an entregamer. Something always falls apart as you are putting your business together. I always say that building a business while having a baby is like swimming while paralyzed. Is it possible? Yeah, but you must be sickly addicted to it like a video game. Because who is going to swim while paralyzed on purpose? No one. Unless they are sick like that. Like us. After three years I ultimately gave up and thought I would have to give up my relationship with my friend as well. I stopped responding to her hate filled texts. At first this made her furious. She had expectations and I was not fulfilling them. She made threats, yelled, insulted and eventually...stopped texting. She no longer talks to me. I am okay with that now that I realized she was indeed trying to hurt me. I do not know if it was jealousy that business to me is fun, so I am successful at it and I have never had to deal with the anxiety that she felt? I do not know, and I do not have the time to analyze it. I must go play another EntreGame.

I have noticed some people feel entitled to success, like, if you put in the work, any work, you will be a success. When really, video games do not care about you. Your business does not care about you either. It laughs in your face when you lose. It is not easy to beat a video game that has all the answers and knows all the moves as you get to die repeatedly until you figure it out. Anyone who starts a business because they think it is easier money than getting a job is always sad when they realize they just put their money into a slot machine, and nothing came back out. Then put more in and still nothing. Then they try some sweat equity and again, nothing. They do not realize it takes money and sweat equity, but it also takes a fever, poison, and a few cheat codes for real money to come out. But this type of hardship does not deter a true EntreGamer. In fact, an EntreGamer does not even think about the end when they play. When a kid opens a new game on Christmas morning…Are they thinking about beating the whole game? No! They are wondering if they will like it and get excited to play. That is the same with an EntreGamer. Will I like this business model? Is this my poison that I just can't stay away from? Just like you do not have to motivate yourself to be ready and play a video game, you do not have to motivate yourself to be an EntreGamer. Just play. It is alright. You will be terrible at it at first. Just like a video game. What do you do when you die in a video game? No self-pity. You restart that game as fast as possible and stomp on that stupid Mario mushroom next time, right?!

Let me ask you an honest question. Do you ever expect to win a video game without practice? No? Then do not expect it with your EntreGame. No practice? No winning. When you get to level 2 are you thinking, 'I'm not on level 10 yet! I'm such a loser.' No! You are likely thinking, "Whew, I made it. I wonder what level 2 is like and what I'm about to face now." It is the same with business. Also, just like playing a video game, no one wants to be around you when you are a poor sport. If you whine and say things like, "No fair! My business should be taking off by now" in Facebook groups or other platforms, people are going to avoid you. No one is going to want to collaborate with you on something cool that could possibly make a lot of money. Like a Super EntreGame that they have been hiding and they are looking for just the right partner. That will not be you if your attitude is like that.

Now, just like there are different video game makers in real life and each one makes different games for different audiences, in your EntreGame, it is the same, but is called 'Business Models'. Different business models are different EntreGames and each one is played a little bit differently. So, examine them like you would when looking for the next video game that you want to buy. Which business model looks fun and that, when you see the poison, you might not mind it? Even if you try one business model and it does not pan out, pick another one. Just by playing different business models, your EntreGame reflexes get better and better each time. Pretty soon, each business model seems like each other but with only minor differences.

So, I have these questions…What do you do when you are playing a video game and you lose hundreds of times, and you just cannot get beyond this one bad guy? What do you do? You go online and look for cheat codes, right? Online courses are those cheat codes for you, and I have a few extra in this book. Want to play an EntreGame with me? Want to discover some cheat codes?

CHAPTER 6

Cheat Code #1

Everything that you know is wrong. The most important cheat code in my arsenal is the 'tune out' button in my brain. Everyone has an opinion based on safe theories, studies, or statistics that they once heard about from some guy wearing a tie on the television, who really knows nothing, but because of it, they really believe it. I used to believe things like that too. Then one day I became so desperate that I tried the thing I always swore I would not. I bought a $197 course from a guy that had a slick radio quality voice and a YouTube channel. After I put his course into action and saw money start to flow in, I realized three things:

1. I have been lied to.
2. Things have changed.
3. No one will ever believe me if I tell them this.

Did his course just work for me and nobody else? Yes and no. Yes, because so many people bought the course and did not actually use it. No, because people who bought the course and put it to action saw results. But it is easy to say that 'paid courses don't work' when you just don't feel like completing them. Over the next seven years after I purchased this course, I thought a lot about people's belief systems and what made them stop believing a paid course would work. Or why basic business principles are seen as voodoo or magic, and you are just lucky if it works. Then one day I stepped into another paid course by Tim Grover. As he spoke, lightning struck my brain, and I realized the answer to that question. Tim Grover did not talk about the subject or have the actual answer but for some reason, while he was talking about who we are as children and about pretending to be someone we are not, it hit me like a ton of bricks. I realized that we believe like that because we are taught that way. No kidding Sherlock, right? I know you are thinking that. But just hear me out. We then each grow up and teach the same thing to others. Yeah? Just wait, it's coming. Most educationars and trainers, they do extremes themselves, but they cannot teach those extremes. A super model who becomes a personal trainer cannot teach her client how to fully go to the extremes that she had endured to become that super model. Why? One word: Liabilities.

If Elon Musk taught a course on how he spent sleepless nights on planes between businesses, constantly working to the point of physical danger...liability. It is the same for everything and everyone. Courses and trainings must be taught the safe way but the people seeing the results do anything but the safe thing. The people seeing the results do not see the end before the first step and the people around them warn them of the safety risks. These people are completely Reckless. So am I. I get the same warnings from my own family. My dad once sat me down in a room to tell me why I did not know anything about my business, and that I was overextending myself while doing everything wrong. He was the one that was wrong. I knew every single number in my business, on every level, and I tracked it every single week. I knew how many leads we were bringing in, the exact conversion percentages, the percentages of people opening the first email versus the fifth email, the percentages of people who signed up for my workshops versus the percentages who purchased at the end. I knew which ads made millions and split test them thousands of times. But when I tried to tell that to my dad, he completely ignored what I said and repeated that I do not know the numbers of my company and how I overextend myself.

Ironically enough, my mom knew this blitz was coming and she just pretended to be asleep on the bed next us while we had our conversation. This conversation took place in a hotel room before I took my dad to a Yankees game. Is my dad a jerk for doing that? No. He was worried about me and my safety. And it did not matter if I had every right answer, it would always be wrong to him because I would always be an eight-year-old girl selling painted rocks on the corner street to him. Would that conversation stop me from being reckless? Nope. In fact, I stopped keeping track of the numbers, made the worst decision in my company's history to implement the wrong program by the wrong mentor, and the entire company went straight into debt and almost went bankrupt.

At that point, I probably should have given up and just got a job. Any sane person would do that. I am not sane. I am reckless. I will not lie, when my company crumbled, I was suicidal at first. Suddenly, running a company became more than a video game. It was my identity. And if it failed, that meant I am a failure too. I should just end it all then. At least that was my thought process, even if I now know that it was wrong of me to think that. Sometimes you cannot help those thoughts. It took me about two long months of self-pity and moping to finally decide I would give it another go. That is when it became a video game again. I mean…I could not do worse than where I was, right? I was at the bottom. The only place to go was up! Though, it did not help that when I decided to try again, I had just gotten pregnant with my 4th child and would be making the decision to work through the pregnancy as well as the baby's childhood. Why did I do it? Am I just that moral breadwinner who must feed the family despite the painful sacrifices of working sixteen-hour days while pregnant? I mean…Within two hours of having a c-section, I was on my phone working again. Am I just an amazing human being who will do anything for my family? Hell no. I am an addicted junky who cannot stay away. Like a moth to a flame, at rock bottom, pregnant, vomiting every few hours from morning sickness, I picked up a new business book that talked about focusing on one thing and one thing only that would fix things. And from there I got an immediate fever and declared I would do another YouTube orbit.

A YouTube Orbit, for those of you who don't know, is when you post one video every single day, for 365 days a year. You do not miss a single day. Your birthday, Christmas, the day you give birth to your baby…yup. Every single day. And I did it. I hit all 365 days and it fixed my company. The days I was sick and pregnant, leading up to the birth when I was swollen with kankles, mid-pandemic when I couldn't even fix my hair, the day I gave birth and every day after that, including the days I had little to no sleep, there was a video planned, recorded, edited and marketed. Who would do that? Only a reckless, crazy, sick person, right? I am that person. But here is the thing. I could never recommend you do the same thing because…liabilities. The reckless parts must be within you, like an addiction. I can only tell you what I did. And if you do it yourself…well…you made that decision on your own, see? After I became reckless and succeeded for the very first time, I started noticing changes in the safe, establishment world. I noticed that many people were choosing to self-publish their books instead of going with big name publishers. The more I looked into my own book to publish, the more I realized what a rip-off publishers are. Publishers only want to work with people who have an audience. Hello! Celebrities, right?!? This way, you pretty much sell your own book to your own followers and the publishers get a cut. Normally, back in the day, the publishers would do all the leg work of editing, printing, and promotion to brick n mortar bookstores, right? I soon learned that publishers expected you to have your own books edited, and then the publishers would print your book with their publishing name, but you were expected to promote your own book to your own following because…no more brick n mortar bookstores. And if you could not get your own book sales? A publisher did not want to work with you.

Wait … what?!? If I must sell my own books to get in with a publisher, why would I want to get in with a publisher and give them a cut for doing nothing but giving me their name to print on my book? And a name that nobody really cares about. With print on demand options, why would anyone in their right mind go with a traditional publisher? My mom wanted to publish a children's book and I told her this. She did not listen. She decided to listen to someone else's advice. This other person told my mom that the correct way to publish a book is to get an agent and then the agent gets in with a big publisher who does the rest. I knew this was the old way of doing things, but my mom listened to this other person, even though this other person did not get the communications degree that I received specializing in publishing. This person has never published a book, never written anything that was published, and did not work anywhere near the industry. In fact, this person worked in the medical industry with doctors and patients. But clearly, my mom thought she was an expert and was convinced that getting an agent was the correct way. My mom announced this to me, and I shrugged, knowing the difficult time she was going to have. But there is no convincing someone that the safe sounding way is wrong.

Doesn't an agent doing all the work for you sound so proper and safe? You will be a success, right? How can you lose when you are going through the correct, safe way? But that is exactly how you lose. Safe is for losers. What happened next was a painful experience for my mom that ultimately took years for her to untangle herself from. My mom got an agent. The agent made my mom sign a contract that she would not publish the book or find any other agents or publishers until he found someone for her and her book. This agent told my mom that it could take years to "shop her book around" to the right publisher. A year later, my mom contacted him, and he said he was still trying and to not give up. Two years later, my mom contacted him, and he said he was still working on it. It was now three years later, and he shrugged it off saying it is not a unique book and publishers were not interested in it. But even after that, he would not let my mom out of her contract. It would be published through him as an agent or not at all. Finally, my mom became reckless. I became so proud of my mom! My mom made the decision to take the same materials and form a new book. Contract loophole? Yes please! And she published it herself, through Print on Demand on Amazon. She did it when she became reckless and stopped listening to the old ways of doing things. My mom has a long journey ahead of her now. She must build an audience.

And wouldn't you know? That is Cheat Code #2!

CHAPTER 7

Cheat Code #2

I have read the most amazing business books that say profit needs to be the primary objective in your company from day one. That sounds cool. But that is not what made me millions. I did not focus on profit until…well I still do not focus on profit. That does not make for a fun video game. Yuck. What made me millions of dollars was putting my audience first right from day one. Growing that audience and serving that audience.

The more generous I am to my business audiences, the more money I make. If I put profit first, ok fine, but I guarantee you that I have more ravenous fans than yours and they trust me more than yours trust you. An audience's first stance answers all the hard questions people ask when starting a business.

- What should I sell?
- What products sell well?
- The better question is…Who?

- Who are you going to serve?
- And what do they want?

How can you give it to them better than anyone else? Or how can you make it better than anyone else? Most people who create products have a hard time coming up with their target audience. In business, this has been called "creating your avatar" or "designing your target market," etc. There have been entire books designed to help business owners with this. Please stop. STOP. You are killing me. You do not need to go that deep to make money.

If you put out a lemonade stand on a hot day, your target market is the people passing by who are thirsty. It can be as simple as that and then you can get to those nitpicky workbooks later. But to get started, pick an audience that you can say in a sentence.

Example: I sell ____________ to ______________.

Or, if you do not know what to sell, then make it an even easier sentence.

I serve ________________.

If you cannot fill that in…well…You are going to struggle forever. I sell soft baby clothes to moms and their babies. I sell Keto Cookbooks to Keto Obsessed Dieters.

You try it!

You can get more into your target market later. But if you have that sentence filled in, then you can start to build an audience. There are two ways to build a buying audience.

BP - Before Product - You can build the audience before offering your product to them.

I have done this via YouTube. You simply show people things that you have learned and what works for you and then they want a premium version of it. This works well for newbies who do not yet know what they want to sell because your audience will start begging you to give you money if you make X product for them. This is a great way to do a product launch because you have an audience waiting impatiently to pay you for your product. However, it can take a lot of building up. It can take a year or more to build up a proper audience for a launch this way. So, you are basically paying your dues and doing all your workload upfront. Not a lot of people like this because there is still no guarantee that people will buy your product. But I do have to say that this way contains the biggest rush ever when you do hit the product out of the park because…it feels like you just hit three 7's on a slot machine and money just starts pouring out. So, if you want a rush, this is the way. Of course, this can also go terribly wrong. I once saw a botched launch go viral where an Instagram Influencer with 2.6 million followers could not sell the required thirty-six t-shirts to put the order into production. My dad told me that this is because sexy influencers with cleavage cannot sell t-shirts. "There is a disconnect", he said. My dad is wrong. I saw another hot Instagrammer make almost $12 million selling her own used bath water. Influencers are the new sales generation. If they cannot sell, it is because they did not ask their audience what they wanted or they are not connecting enough with their audience to know. It would be like going into Best Buy to purchase a television and the sales guy keeps showing you the laptops.

The Instagrammer selling the t-shirts put what she wanted on it and not what her audience wanted. If she had connected with her audience, polled them, and asked "which one of these do you like? A, B or C? Vote!" Then narrow down the options according to what her audience wanted, and then they would have ultimately purchased more. Or…she could have just sold her bath water like the other Instagrammer. Either way, even with putting cleavage shots on Instagram, if you build a following of 2.6 million people, you can find something to sell to them that they would like. You just need to find out what that is. If instead, you want a little less risk in a botched launch and a little more dripped income upfront, then you want to go with an AP way of building an audience, After Product.

AP - After Product - You can build your product offer and build your audience after your products are in place for them to buy.

This requires building two or more products upfront. You need to build the product or product line that you want your customers to buy, and you also need a free sample to get them in. Think of the chocolate store in the mall. Have a free sample! Good! Now buy a pound! It works the same way with this business model. I have done this successfully by bringing customers in via free product samples. For example, "Here's a free hardcover cookbook! Now get in on the meal planning app for a two-week free trial!" And then, ultimately, after trying the products, they pay for the app subscription. This has also worked for courses. I have offered a free digital class or training and then at the end, I offer the premium version. Or for an ecommerce-based business model, you do not even have to offer a free sample. You can offer a discount code and it can have the same effect. In fact, statistics show that the #1 way to generate leads for an ecommerce-based business model is to offer a discount in exchange for a customer's email address or text number.

But through any of the things we just talked about, you are leading your customers in through something called a sales funnel or sales pipeline. No funnel or pipeline to capture your customers? No orders. With the AP business model approach, after you build out your free product to your paid product offer, you need to start doing ads or promos with a generic audience and then narrow your way in when you start seeing results and who you are attracting.

My dad used to go fishing and when he arrived, he would always ask the other fishermen, "What are you using for bait? What are they biting?" Then my dad would use the same thing. All you need is the general fishpond to start with. Remember the fill in the blank? I sell _________ to __________. So, I would build out my products and then start sending ads to the general pond to see what people are biting on. What bait will work first?

You could also look at what your competitors are doing for ads. Use similar bait if it looks like it is working. But obviously with your own spin, brand, and products. When people start biting the bait, every ad software known to existence automatically tracks the demographics of whose biting, except Etsy. Etsy is kind of dumb. But all the ad agencies, ad companies themselves like Facebook, Instagram, Pinterest and Google, they build out those workbooks for you. You do not have to lift a finger; you do not have to fill out a workbook. Once people start biting and you get that additional information about the people who are biting, you can make your ads even better and test them against your older ads to see if you can beat yourself with a cheaper bait and cheaper bite on your ads. --Competing against yourself is the most fun video game of all.

But with all of this, this is just the bite. How do you reel the customer in once they bite the bait? How can you turn that bite into a dollar?

That is our next cheat code.

CHAPTER 8

Cheat Code #3

When I decided to acquire a new company, I went to the best of the best, Empire Flippers. Yes, there are other websites that sell companies, but I personally prefer Empire Flippers because they do all the vetting for me. After I bought another business previously from a competitor of Empire Flippers, I realized it was a big mistake and had to do a lot of leg work with a whole staff to update things and make that business work. I was heartbroken. I had been doing business for years and questioned everything I knew after I was taken by this seller. *Maybe I am really a failure because I did not see this red flag. Maybe I should just quit?* I thought.

After experiencing a proper vetting service, looking back, I would not have seen this red flag myself or knew the right questions to ask. But a proper vetting service would have. So now, when I acquire something new, I like to go through Empire

Flippers as an agency. I think of them like the IRS. They get all up in the seller's business and make sure everything is legitimate before Empire Flippers will even sell it. Empire Flippers have a high rejection rate, and they reject selling most businesses that come to them. Very few businesses make it through the entire vetting process. Now I know that, if Empire Flippers would have seen the company I acquired from a competitor, it would have been amongst the rejects. Simply put, Empire Flippers are the best out there and I would not acquire a company from anyone else. At the same time though, I disagree with Empire Flippers' valuation models and numbers. How can this be when I think they are the best of the best? Here is the thing. I disagree, but I understand why they grade things the way they do, and I also benefit from the disagreement so I would not want them to change it. Let me explain.

People who truly know how to make money in business know that the value of the company is in the list. When Disney acquired Marvel for $4 billion in 2009, that valuation was not that high because of the quality of the movies, the script writing, or the assets. It was that high because of the list. Marvel had a huge fan base and all the tracking, email addresses, Facebook pages and more of those fans. Disney paid $4 billion for Marvel's list and the assets to continually sell more products to that list. Disney could have easily made movies to compete with Marvel. They have the budget. So why wouldn't they? Because Marvel had the list. But there are certain strategies that I and most entrepreneurs had to learn the hard way to use that list and make offers in such a way that folks will purchase. I got my business in trouble again financially from being reckless, and so I got out a big sheet of paper and started making a new million-dollar plan to get out of it. This time, my children were 11, 12 and 16. They were old enough for me to explain to them how I make money. So, as I built the plan, I would ask them questions just to see how they responded or what they would do. I wrote out the plan and I said to my 11-year-old. Hmmm, "How should we get the plan out to our audience? Should we just do YouTube and social media?" She said "Yup!" Then I asked, "Should we send emails?" I was shocked at her answer, but I should not have been. Her answer is the same answer I get from 99% of business owners when I ask this question. My 11-year-old said, "No, because most people don't like email and they'll find it annoying." To this I replied, "Hmmm, okay. But just so you know, this is the #1 way we make the money is if we send these emails. We will probably make 1% of what we would make if we do not send the emails. Should we still not send emails because they're annoying?' My 11-year-old changed her answer immediately and said, "Send the emails!!" Even an 11-year-old gets it. But still...Some business owners get all weird and self-righteous about email marketing. Like they have more integrity than the next business because they do not annoy people with emails. But an email list is more than an email list, especially in recent times. Email lists can be uploaded to Facebook, Instagram, Pinterest, and Google so you can target ads to your audience. You can also ask Facebook or similar ad companies to make something called 'look-a-like audiences' with your list. Facebook does all the work to find out your target market from your uploaded list and will send your ads to people exactly like those already on your list. From my experience, this one feature of Facebook ads is what made me that first million. And I could not have done it without an email list. So, to me, an email list is the most important part in the valuation of acquiring a company.

Back to Empire Flippers. They do not take much value in an email list. Why? Well, I have one theory, but I did not actually ask them. They brag that they sell businesses that pretty much run themselves. An email list, sending emails, knowing what emails to send that will make money…that takes a certain knowledge that does not come free on YouTube, and it takes a honed skill as well. Empire Flippers wants to sell a business that is almost completely automated. So, in what I have studied of their valuations, the more automated a company, the more it is worth and the more it costs you. Okay I understand that. But an entrepreneur with any amount of experience running a company knows that this way of evaluating a company is completely based on Amazon PPC ads and you are not actually gathering an email list. You are just selling on Amazon and not capturing any of those leads which is as risky as it comes. Amazon shuts down your account and you have nothing left. But if I have a list, I can move to other platforms and as new ad platforms pop up, I can bring new people in on any social media platform that pops up in the future. Bottom line is if I have a list, I can be reckless, take more risks, and reap more rewards. This is because if I screw up, I know how to hustle to create something for that audience that they would find irresistible. This is not dishonest. You are providing a service. You are simply the ice cream man in the truck circling the neighborhoods to get ice cream into the hands of the children. But if that ice cream man does not have a neighborhood to circle in...then what? You need a list.

The first company I acquired from Empire Flippers was valued far below many of the other companies and I felt as though I struck gold. This company had an email list of 4,000 followers. It was automated as well but I could not figure out why the value of this company and a lot of other companies that have lower valuations, are the ones with email lists. And the companies with higher valuations do not have little to no list at all most of the time. But this is just one of those things that, because you want something automated so you can do less work, you will pay more. And because I am willing to work recklessly and play the video game, I will take the lower valued company with the list, compete against your little automated number, and win every time.

I have found the biggest rookie mistake people make when they build any business model from scratch is when they spend all their time creating and no time selling or marketing what they created. People do not realize that every product has a full lifecycle. Just like people and animals! A product is born, it matures, it declines. Thus, many people make a product and kind of post about it, then they do not get a huge reaction and they move onto the next product. People will post on social media where nobody cares and ignore the number one money-making way of email marketing, because it might annoy people. Do you know why emails annoy people and social media does not? Because they do not have to pay attention to you on social media. But your emails get right in front of their face. That is what you want! And if they do not want that then they can utilize the unsubscribe button.

One of the other reasons business owners might shy away from an email list is because most email software has become ridiculously complex. I used to use complex email software thinking I had to know everything and use all the features to make money. I soon realized that I did not need any of those bells and whistles. I just wanted something simple. In most of the email software, I had to learn the lingo and go through tutorials before I could even send an email. Yuck. I used to ask, "Where's the 'send an email' button?" That is all I want! Eventually, I created OHWO, the simplest email marketing software out there. It takes a minute to set up your domain email, but after that, guess what? You just look for the InstaMail button or the 'Send an Email' button in the left side menu. I built OHWO for myself, but you can use it too. This is because it is the simplest and the least expensive out there. You might as well give it a go if you have never tried email marketing. I have canceled all my other email marketing software and now exclusively use my own. You will never convince me to go back to being complicated. I make the same amount of money when I use simple rather than when I use complex. So, the money from a company's email list is not in the software of the email list. It is in what you email.

But wait...You know you need an email list. But what are those strategies to make an email list valuable and work if it is not in the email marketing software? What are the secrets that get the money out of the list?

Welp, that is Cheat Code #4.

CHAPTER 9

Cheat Code #4

I once bought a course on search engine optimization, and right in the middle of it, Brad Callen, I will never forget, said something that changed my entire business forever. And it was about email lists. He was showing how you bring people in through a search engine but then he showed an email on his screen and said, "This is an automated email." He explained that when people sign up for your list, you should send a welcome automated email. And then he said the bomb that changed my world. He said that some people set up one or two automated emails like this and then they are done. He said, "Why are you working like that? Set up and send HUNDREDS of automated emails."

My brain exploded. This was a completely reckless idea. Who would do this? Who would put in this amount of work? This is when I created something years ago that I call "The Renae Christine Experience" to this day. It's not just hundreds of automated emails. It is 180 days' worth of an entire experience. From one email to the next, they tie all together like a theme park. There is the whirly, twirly roller coaster over there, and there is the cotton candy booth over there. These are not sales emails. These are delicious emails that help my audience. With these set up, anyone entering my system gets to go on all of the rollercoasters while I get to know them. And as I get to know them, I see what they like and don't like. This is when I build or find a cool product that I know they would love and pay for. By this time, they have experienced such awesome free help from my automated emails that they are begging me to let them into my premium version of the park.

I once paid close to $20,000 to be mentored by David Siteman Garland, the coach who got me to my first million during that same year. DSG was much bigger than me but when I invited my audience to meet him, my audience started breaking things. My audience clicks with such ferocity that every webinar software in existence has broken. We have also broken every website when we are all trying to click on the same thing. My sales and sign-up pages are so abused that once a rumor circulated how I make the pages crash on purpose as a marketing technique. Are you kidding me? The whole point of the whole Renae Christine Experience is to get you to click that final button on the sales page. Who would crash the page to make it so you can't get to the one step we want you to get to? My mentor experienced this and asked me, "Renae, what makes your fans so rabid?" He said he has been around the block with the best and none of their fans are that crazy. He's never seen anything like it. I simply told him, "It's the Renae Christine Experience." Give one sample of chocolate and they buy a pound. So how much more will they buy if you give them ten pounds for free? Most coaches would say this is a ridiculous analogy. They would say If you gave them ten pounds then they are full and will not want anymore. They will be sick of it and won't buy anything else. Keep thinking that because I'm about to steal your list. The more generous I am with my experience, the more people buy later. But wait... what could be in these emails and could you really do something similar? Allow me to spill one of the most valuable lessons I learned from another email marketing training that I paid for. I spent about $247 for this training and there were three things that I learned that made the entire cost of the course worth it. These three things are the true secrets behind the entire Renae Christine Experience.

It doesn't matter what your products are or what industry you are in, this will change the way you think of email marketing and all your blank ideas will be filled with your own version of your own experience.

#1. Write PS at the bottom of your emails for the most important thing that you want people to get from your email. Most people don't read an entire email. They skim to look at images and they read the titles or bolded text. Then there are some fans who read every word. But there is one thing that everyone reads and that is the PS at the bottom. I don't know how to explain it psychologically. But people assume your email is what you want them to read. A PS is an afterthought that people think you do not want to be important, so they make it important. When I make an email for my experience, I always include the most important thing with a link as a PS at the very bottom.

#2. Train people to read the PS in one of your very first welcome emails…through a PS. In your welcome email, put a PS at the bottom that says something like 'I put the most important information at the bottom in a PS so watch out for that!' You are acknowledging your audience's busy schedule and lack of time for reading. So that PS is like sending a text. This will make more people open your emails because they can quickly look at the PS. And then for the fans who read the PS and want to read more, they will skim back up to the top of the email and start to read.

#3. Do PS, PPS, PPPS and fill the PPS and PPPS with something called a Soap Opera Sequence. The first PS should be the action that the reader can take in the email that you are writing about. This is not always very sales oriented. It can be something like 'take a look at my favorite list of …' or 'download my favorite …' The PPS and PPPS should be part of a Soap Opera Sequence. What is a Soap Opera Sequence? Did you ever watch a Soap Opera and nothing ever seemed to be resolved but it was at the same time? How do they do that cliffhanger on Friday afternoon where you think everything is about to unravel and on Monday they tie it back up to what it was on Friday? I don't know about you, but this kept me watching Days Of Our Lives for years as a teenager. Hope and Bo forever!

How this works is you first write about something coming up in your experience. Remember, we're planning out an entire experience so you should know what you are going to email next and get people excited about it. I will sometimes ask a question in the PPS and say that I am gathering some more fun things and will send it soon. For Example: PPS. Did you want to see my all-time favorite go-to business books that I put away for my kids in case I die? These are that important! I will gather those up and send them to you soon. Watch your email so you don't miss it.

I know that is a long PPS. Sometimes I will make it longer or shorter. And then I get six emails ready with six different business books that I plan on giving to my kids when I die. One in each email and at the bottom of each email is a PPS touting the next one.

PPS. I have another business book that I am giving my children when I die but it is a little more controversial. I will go grab it for you. Watch for the email. You will love this one.

After the PPS we then have the PPPS. Sometimes I include this and sometimes I don't. If I have the PPS to bring people into the next email and wait for it, I do not necessarily have to have a PPPS. However, I like to use the PPPS to teach something about something I might sell in the future. Sometimes, if you are going to give someone an offer, they naturally reject it unless you have overcome objections before you even show them the offer. I know that sounds confusing but what if I told you I created this ice cream that had zero calories in it before you even knew what it was called or that I was even offering it? It might pique your interest before you have a chance to turn it away. If I put something on my kids' plates to eat, they automatically don't want it. But if they see me eating it and not wanting to give them any, they want some. It is the same psychology. So, I might say something like this:

PPPS. My paid course is opening soon, and I get so many questions asking about it. Do not pay any attention to that right now because it is closed, and I just want to spoil you with free things right now.

This creates an insane reaction of 'What?!? You're telling me NO?!? This is so unfair!' Don't think this really works? I did this to the extreme with a training bonus I used to give out. Until now I have never publicly admitted that I did this. I have since had to disband this additional experience because the secret got out and people started demanding it before they bought it.

Confused?

This is how it worked.

I had two premium trainings called Handmade Titan University and Architect. Both cost between $997 - $1997 each depending on the season or bonuses packaged with it. When someone would buy one of my premium trainings for $997, I would send an email after thirty days saying that I heard everyone was interested in the second premium program, but it is closed, and you have to wait but that the second program cost $997. Shortly after that, I sent an email requesting a mailing address so I could send a little welcome packet for the premium program they purchased thirty days ago.

It is important that all of this happened thirty days after their purchase because anyone who refunded the program within thirty days would not learn about the surprise I was about to send them. I did not want their purchase decision to be based on the welcome packet I was sending. The welcome packet that I sent reduced people to tears. Within the welcome packet was a note that swore them to secrecy on what was inside the packet. I also had an entire staff who deleted any posts in our Facebook group spilling details about what was in the packet. So, people would wait thirty days, fill out this form, get this welcome packet, and many would burst into tears. They would post selfies of themselves crying in our Facebook group. Because of this, others would be really interested in this welcome packet. It can't be that great! But still, they fill out their mailing address to get one too. Even the most skeptical customers ended up crying and posting on Facebook that they were making fun of the previous criers but cried themselves when they saw what was in the welcome packet. From here, people started filling out their mailing address and stalking the mailman. One person put a lawn chair out next to her mailbox and sat there each day until it came. And then she too ended up in tears.

This madness went on for years until the secret of the welcome packet finally got out and we had to end the program. What was in the welcome packet? It was a golden ticket to the other premium course for free. So, if someone purchased Handmade Titan University for $997, they got the $997 Architect training for free, or vice versa. This was all a fabulous Renae Christine Experience until our customers started spilling the secret in Facebook groups and people started contacting us before purchasing stating they only wanted the program if it came with the welcome packet with the other course. Suddenly, it was no longer a welcomed surprise, it was a demanded entitlement before purchasing. We had no choice but to end the program, but it was spectacular while it lasted. Here is why this experience worked for those few years. That email with the PS. The email said we are getting a lot of questions about our other training that it is closed but we will tell you that it costs $997. That email made the tears, not the delivery of the welcome packet itself or what was inside the packet. Everyone reading that email before receiving the packet thought I was about to sell them another course and they got a sick feeling in their gut. This happens all the time, right? Some guru sells you a course, you get in then they sell you another one.

So, I played into that and made them feel sick. Sorry, not sorry! This sick feeling from that email's PS is what led to a surprise and thus…tears and the stalking of mailmen. The PS soap opera sequences can produce emotion in an email where you cannot do that above the PS or on social media. Use it. Make your theme park. Make your own experience. Don't just put up one automated email. Put up hundreds! Now, we are working on additional Renae Christine Experiences with other companies and processes to get similar reactions elsewhere. It takes a lot of time getting those hundreds of emails up. But it makes for a less risky company with an audience that will last for the rest of your life if you want it to. It is not hard to think about what type of experience to write up. Think of our kids. I once told my daughter that she was going to the doctor to get shots. I delivered her to a surprise party at a resort with a pool. Think torture then surprise! Again, sorry, not sorry! Now, setting up these automated emails that fancy people call autoresponders, can take time. It can take as much time as writing a book can take time. So how do you get it all done?

You must do what I do, which I'll show you in the next cheat code.

CHAPTER 10

Cheat Code #5

You get balance, or you get a business. You cannot have both. The sooner you accept this, the more you can focus on obsessing over your business guilt-free or...semi guilt-free. Okay, the guilt is still there but you can pretend you are guilt free.

I once paid $997 for a Mental Toughness 8-week program by Tim Grover. The biggest thing that I learned is that I'm not the only one who feels guilty about wanting to do big things. I thought, maybe because I'm a woman or a mom, maybe that is why I feel guilty about wanting to prioritize my business. Then I learned from the men in the program that it is not a gender reduced feeling. Men feel just as much guilt. But tend to be quieter about it and usually they have an excuse as breadwinners to work that hard. No fair! I also learned that no one in that group has any sort of balance. All of them are as reckless as I am. I loved this program because it was real about the guilt you feel but also that you have to work while feeling the guilt. What a reckless notion that would never be in a millionaire habits book. It is hard to sell a millionaire habits book if you have to talk about getting over guilt. It is better to say safe things like "balance is good" or "write down your goals before bedtime." When in reality, the person who wrote that book does none of those things and feels guilty as hell for having to work while his wife and kids miss him. He just doesn't want to talk about it. He will close his eyes and pretend he lives the book he wrote. They all say the same things to their wives as I say to my husband. "I'm sorry. I just have to do this," and I get back to work.

Unfortunately, a work addiction is like a drug addiction. It actually feeds your family, so it has a potential to be stronger than any drug because your entire lifestyle depends on it. Once, my disabled husband was trying to change our baby's clothes. His disability made it difficult for him to do so while the baby squirmed to get away, he lost his temper. The baby became scared and began to cry. Did I blame my husband? Nope. I felt like it was my fault because I was working while it happened. I felt guilty because I should have been the one changing the diaper. I know that I work too much. I would work every single waking second if I could possibly do so. Is it that I want to avoid my kids and my husband? Absolutely not! I love my family and I want my husband to sit next to me while I work. He can do the things he loves to do on his phone or computer, and I can do the things I love (work). We can do it right next to each other and have our private chef cook us steaks and the nanny change the diapers. Yeah! Doesn't that sound like the greatest video game of all?!?

Where does balance come into the picture of that video game? Nowhere. Because if you stop to change the diaper or make the steaks, you make less money. Bye-bye private chef. Bye-bye nanny. And I am not really saying the end goal is to have a private chef or nanny. But I am saying those things help you to play your video game even more. So, if it is about playing your video game more, then those are important enablers for that. Balance is really the opposite of success. Does the hero of a video game ever stop to take a nap because he or she needs balance? No! They become absolutely obsessed and cannot do anything else. They are also usually single without kids because there is no way to do it all while married and having children. I think the hero should get married, have kids, get a private chef, nanny and oh yes! A maid. There! He is all set to obsess and get it all. I know. I sound like a selfish narcissistic psychopath. I just think there is always a way to be surrounded by the people you love and do the things you are obsessed with doing. There is nothing wrong with paid help to make that happen. All of this starts with...wait for it...a supportive family.

Man or woman, how do you get your family to truly support what you want to do? Because you are ultimately asking them to take on more responsibilities if you are working all the time, right? If you are working all the time, it means you can't help with the dishes. And you have not made the money for that maid yet, right? It is like the chicken and the egg. Do you work to get the maid, or do you get the maid so you can work? Also, sometimes your spouse and kids actually want to do things with you such as play games, go to the movies, go on vacation, and things like that. You and your family have to accept that your life will be different if you choose this path. You all must agree on the dream. This is the dream house, dream location, dream cars, dream schools (or homeschool), and dream habits. Now, I did not actually get my family to agree on anything. I just delivered by making more money. We need a bigger house so I can have a YouTube studio to make more money! Bam! And now the family is completely addicted to that larger home, and they don't want to downsize ever again. This means that I have to keep working to stay in that house. Oh darn. I guess I have to keep working now. The family will understand and be supportive. (Insert evil smiley face here).

When you are just starting out on this new reckless path then I invite you to borrow my go-to catchphrase. When I have to keep working and other people are having a hard time because they are sitting in the middle of dishes or unwashed clothing, then you just say the following: "I'm sorry. I just have to do this." They might still be mad at you. But eventually they will come around as their lives improve and they do not want to downgrade after you deliver. Are you buying their love? No. But you are buying more time to work. You will still feel guilty, but you will learn to work through it. Think of it like bribery or blackmail so you can work harder and more often. I know, I sound really sick right now. And I am not done yet. When I upgraded our home, cars, and my husband's toys, we had bigger bills, right? A lot of people cringe at this, but this makes me quite happy because now I have an excuse to work and play my video game even more. Oh! And soon I will also have a nanny. That is my next plan so I can obsess even more. Is this all so wrong? Yep. Do not care. I have got to play more.

If all of this makes you put on a disgusted face because you refuse to put your family second or you refuse to work all the time because that's not what you want for your life, then none of this is for you. None of it. Put the book down. Enjoy your secure job with pizza every Friday night as your bonus. You will not be able to compete against anyone else in the business arena because you will hate this, they are ALL like me. It is a video game for all of them. How can you win at a video game that you only play an hour a day and the guy next to you is playing every waking moment? You can't. So, quit. Was I always this way? I didn't think I was. But I think I was and just never wanted to admit it. I did not have labels for my erratic behavior or addictions. Eventually, it was actually the people around me who acted a certain way that clued me in. For example, my mom would come to town and stay with me for two weeks. I think I left my computer three times while she was there. Wrong, right? So wrong! But my mom so lovingly enabled me and said, "Don't get up. You keep doing what you're doing, and I'll be next to you on MY computer." YES! I love my mom. She has her own video games, and she also plays until she wins. Then I traveled to see my mom at her place. I stayed for two weeks and got up from my computer like three times again. Different room, same situation. My little sister appallingly said, "Is that all you ever do is work on your computer?" At the time I defended myself just like an addict would. "I do not! I mean…I have a family to feed! I mean…I get out sometimes!" I said, with the palest of white skin that had not seen the sun in three years. It was practically translucent. My first husband once laughed at me during a project when I said, "I'm so tired. After I'm done with this, I'm going to relax for a while." He laughed right out loud and said, "Yeah right." Again, I defended myself. 'What do you mean? I can relax! I don't work all the time! I mean…I'm trying to feed the family!' Now I realize that everyone around me saw what I saw last. I am obsessed, reckless and cannot be stopped. Now I know why my mom gave me the nickname 'get-out-of-the-way-Renae'. And when I babysat my five other siblings, she nicknamed me 'Sarge'. I used to be offended by those things. Now, I have given into the dark side, and I agree, just get out of the way. Sarge is coming through.

Ironically, I thought I could control this part of my identity. When I met Tom, the love of my life, I was shy and barely spoke. I was so afraid that he would know what was underneath. No guy really wants a Sarge girlfriend or wife. Eventually though… just like Cruella Deville, it was my identity and it slowly leaked out, bad driving and all. Now, Tom imitates and teases me when I say that maybe I should slow down. He says that if I ever tried to slow down, eventually I would break down and say, in his best Renae voice, "I'm going crazy! I can't stand this!" and then I would build something else.

Tom's brothers also know this, though I tried to hide it from them also. They would be talking about some pipe dream, and I would look at them a certain way, just thinking, and they would stop me short and say, "Don't even think about it, I know that look in your eyes." I didn't even say a word. They just know.

Tom's brothers are awesome. They are very forgiving of my reckless obsession. Thank goodness Tom and his brothers have as many problems as me in other areas so they have no choice but to forgive me. So, when I say "I'm sorry. I just have to do this," they don't try to talk me out of it. This is good because we probably could not get along if they did. The only thing worse than a millionaire habits book talking about balance is a millionaire habits book talking about goals.

Enter the next cheat code.

CHAPTER 11

Cheat code #6

My biggest pet peeve of all in business is when anyone, a coach, student, online guru, article, journalist, talks about goals. The truth is people who tout goals in public are less likely to complete them. Don't believe me? Look at actual studies of people who post their goals on social media.

Hello! New Year's Resolutions! It is common sense as well as proven. The studies say that, when you say the goal out loud or to other people that you get a shot of dopamine as if you already accomplished it, so you do not have to actually go through the hard steps of accomplishing it. I have never said an online goal out loud. I will keep a goal to myself until I am almost through with it and then I can tell people about it. In fact, the word goal is forbidden in our home. I'm serious. My kids, my husband, his family, do not use the word goal. Instead, we use the word plan. When you tell a plan, it is different from a goal. A plan is the work and path to that goal. The goal comes naturally if the plan is secure. Goals produce unnecessary pressure and suck the fun out of everything. I don't hate the word goal because, most likely, those who say a goal out loud do nothing about it. I hate the word goal because nothing associated with it is awesome or fun. When someone starts a video game, do they say, "My goal is to finish this whole video game in three weeks." No! No one says that! And if you do, you are a loser. You need to have fun with your journey and your plans. I never have deadlines until a product is completely finished. This is always the most common question asked me by friends, family, business associates, and partners. When we start a project they ask, 'Which date are you thinking to have this done by?'

Or

"When do you think we'll launch this?"

I have the same answer for all of them. No dates. Damn the torpedoes, full steam ahead. I already work every second of the day, what more do you want? If I give myself a date and I'm done early, I will unnecessarily stretch it out. If I give myself a date and I'm not done in time, I will kill myself while at the same time knowing that I worked every second to get it done and it still was not complete. As a reckless workaholic, you do not need deadlines because the right deadline will come naturally as you work away. Repeat after me, "Damn the torpedoes. Full steam ahead!"

I once had a joint venture partnership where I would sell another coach's premium training to my own audience. The owners of the premium training would do a free webinar for my audience, sell their premium training at the end, and that was that. We had this partnership for a few years. And then, one day, it was over. Why? They gave me a goal sheet. No, I'm not kidding. We were getting ready to do a launch and they showed me this worksheet with dollar signs on it. They said that worst case scenario, they would accept Goal #3, but they were really hoping that we would hit Goal #1. This put an unimaginable amount of pressure on me as business models like this run on the rule of averages. I knew I would have to work harder than ever before to get the amount of people to the webinar to achieve the numbers that they wanted. That killed all the fun. Money is not fun. Goals are not fun. Deadlines are not fun.

#NotMyVideoGame.

Bye!

I never worked with them again. When I worked with one of my own favorite mentors, David Siteman Garland, on a similar joint venture project, I was more nervous because DSG was so much bigger than me. I wanted to impress him, and I knew my audience was not as big as his. When I told him this, he told me a line that I have never forgotten and still repeat at least three times a week, every week to myself. I told him I was nervous that our launch would not be as big as his normal launches and DSG said, "You know Renae, worst case scenario, we make money." And then we had an enormous launch and I continue to tout his training to this day, even though he sold it to a colleague of ours. No pressure? Now THAT'S a fun video game. Then I can play on curiosity. Would it not be ridiculous if we did this launch and made a few dollars too? Isn't that fun? But if you give me a goal, a deadline, or any work-related worksheets then I hate you and you could leave. Forever!

I play video games at full steam ahead and say, worst case scenario, we make money. Who cares about the rest? And THAT'S the true mindset that makes millionaires. How many people have said, "If I could just taste-test for a living, I would be so happy" or "If I could play video games for a living, that would rock!' Guess what?!? You can! Damn the torpedoes, full steam ahead.

Everyone who says life and work are not fun have lied to you. If you pick the right poison, go full steam ahead and have the philosophy that worst case scenario, we make money, it is unimaginably fun and addicting. Doesn't that sound like the ultimate video game? One that has real coins come out. I call them fun tickets, but I am pretty sure I heard that somewhere and stole it. While you are dreaming of possibilities, I know coaches and trainers will say that goals are important so you can measure things and know when you are successful…blah blah blah. Then other coaches say, it is important to visualize success and that if you can visualize success then you can be successful. Theodore Roosevelt said, "Believe you can and you're halfway there." I used to teach the same thing. But then I realized something. I never thought I could do anything that I actually did. If you ask most people who were more successful than their wildest dreams, they never believed they could get there. In fact, most failures believed they could, and they couldn't. I thought I couldn't, and I could. How did it happen? I start every project by telling my husband,

"Wouldn't it be ridiculous if this actually worked? How hilarious would that be!" And when it works out, it is like winning a video game. I'm shocked and excited and then I turn to my husband and say, 'Isn't it ridiculous that it turned out this way? So crazy!' And it is because it's a video game without entitlement that got me there.

I wanted to go for the big-time video game, Amazon. Now THAT'S the video game I want to play. That's my poison. You think if I win the Amazon video game that I will make money? Who can say "No" to that? So…full steam ahead! Worst case scenario, we make money. And wouldn't it be ridiculous if we could actually get to the top of Amazon?!? So much fun! What's your video game? What are you going to go full steam ahead on? What would be ridiculous if you could pull it off? Because… worst case scenario, you make money! And if you can learn to make small money, you can learn to make big money.

Allow me to explain in the next cheat code.

CHAPTER 12

Cheat Code #7

"Those aren't typical results," people kept saying in the Facebook group. After I scaled my company to its first million, everyone in David Siteman Garland's Facebook group thought I was some sort of unicorn or freak. They would not listen to me when I tried to tell them that, first, I could not believe it myself, but also that they could do the same thing. I was not doing anything different than my first launch where I made around $3,000. I just used the same strategy and included more people.

If you sell lemonade at a stand in an abandoned neighborhood versus Times Square, what happens, right? You might get the same percentage ratios of sales but there are obviously more people in Times Square. I kept saying this, but nobody believed me. They thought I had some sort of magic button I was not telling them about. I simply built out my business model, remember the Renae Christine experience? And after I found what worked and I learned my percentages, I simply put it in front of more of the same people who were buying, and money started pouring in. I always say, "If you can make a dollar, you can scale it to a million." Period. But you must first learn how to make that dollar.

So many people know the cliche that it "takes money to make money." But most people have five dollars in their wallet. Why are they not using it to make money? Oh wait…it takes a LOT of money to make money? Ok, you do not know what you are talking about then. I know a woman who inherited $500,000 from her father's passing. Is that enough money to make money? She spent it on renovating a home that she later had to abandon, and it would not sell for anything close to what she put into it. She had to downsize into another home that was falling apart. The situation became so messy that this woman eventually moved into a trailer to live out the remainder of her days. So, what happened? I thought you needed a lot of money to make money. Listen, you need ANY money to make money. If you cannot make money from a little bit of money, then you will not know how to make money from the bigger money either.

When people get tax refunds, what do they spend it on? That is money to make money. What do they do? They spend it on vacations, televisions, and other experiences or tech gadgets. What happened to that money? I thought you said that if you had money then you would be able to make money? It turns out, money does not grow from money unless you know how to grow it, small or large. If you educate yourself on the small stuff, the big stuff is easy. Some people call this "Financial Literacy", but it is more than that if you want to run a business. If you want to run a business then you need Financial Literacy, Business Literacy, and Reckless Literacy.

Business literacy is what most people lack when they go to acquire a business. They purchase the business expecting it to run itself, then that person runs the business into the ground and blames the previous owner, or somebody else. When I purchased that botched business, all the numbers looked good. According to anyone financially literate, it looked good! And my business literacy also said it looked good. But when I started running it, I realized the website with over 5,000 products was completely outdated with discontinued products. I had to have my entire staff contact each supplier to get brand new lists and update the entire thing. It took more than six months of staff working full time to get the website where it should have been when it was handed to me. Because I had business literacy, I made it work and I can still make it work if there is a problem. But if someone acquires a business and something goes wrong, well, that is why running a business is considered the riskiest investment. However, when I was looking into real estate investing, I opted to use those extra funds for multiple businesses instead. For me because I am business literate, it is less risky than real estate investing.

I have the skills and I have done it multiple times, and where it might still be risky, investing in anything else would be riskier because of my lack of education in those areas. If you build your knowledge and skills in business and learn how to grow money through a business, that is the key to unlocking millions. Scaling is not as hard as everyone makes it out to be. It is simply hard for you to imagine the ridiculousness of it all. I had a hard time too, even after it happened. All you must do though, is play the video game. Play the video game and when money comes out, you are doing it right. Try to do that again and multiply your progress. Adapt and make changes as problems come. Yes, problems will always come. What video game does not have a villain or two? Play it like a video game, get through the villains and level up. The money will come out. And as you grow more and more, you will get faster and better, and then you too will scale to millions. But you cannot scale to millions until you play the video game enough to know that putting in five dollars can make ten come out. That information is all in the numbers as you build. I am not particularly a fan of the numbers, but you can automate that so someone delivers the numbers to you on a silver platter so you can say, "Hmm, let me make this change over here. Okay that looks good...Continue on and scale up over here."

When I build out a business though, it can take me a year or more of playing a video game before getting to the point of the numbers on a silver platter. Yes, it can take that long to build out an infrastructure where money comes out. But, once it does ... the scaling part is easy. That is why you work extremely hard just to get a dollar. Get the dollar, then scale to a million.

You do not have to believe me; just play the video game and you will be as shocked as I was.

CHAPTER 13

Be Awful

My mom taught piano growing up. She used to tell each new student, "You have to be willing to be bad before you can be good." Each student would plunk their way through their first lesson. My mom always gave me challenging music to the point that I would break down in tears. "I can't play this mom! I can't!" She would make me learn the song anyway which I am now grateful that she did. I would have the song learned by the following week and it would be fun to play. She would follow it up with the next song that made me cry. "You say this every week Renae! And then you learn the song and can play it!" I would reply, "But mom! This one is different! I can't play this one!" And the cycle would go round and round for years.

Anything new that I learned after this, I would keep the same philosophy. Be bad at first, pay your dues, eat crow, then climb unsuspectingly slowly to the top. Most people do not even know

I exist until I am at the top of something. Then they all say the same thing, "Who is this Renae person?" It has happened in every industry that I have tackled. I let my numbers do the talking and you should do the same. But you cannot have good numbers unless you have bad, embarrassing numbers first. Numbers that are not anyone else's business. Numbers that you can hide if you do not go and announce your goals! Announce your success and numbers when you hit the top and make everyone say, "Wait…I didn't even know you were into that Renae!" Surprise! I was playing the video game this whole time and you did not even know. Like a true, embarrassing addiction, keep it in your closet while you are bad.

If you feel you have to announce what you are doing to get support, you are making a huge mistake because first, nobody is going to support you. They are going to worry about you and talk you out of it. And announcing your goal will make you feel like you have attained some success even though you have not done anything yet which will cause you to not move forward. Think about it...A gamer does not announce a goal of how many video games they are going to play that week. They just can't stay away from it. They play a bad game until they are good. Everyone starts bad. Nobody starts off winning a video game the first time through. So why do they keep playing despite being bad? Because they are having fun. If they don't like a game, they'll pick another.

It is the same with business. If you have to be encouraged and motivated after you fail in business, you probably need a different brand of poison. When I'm playing my video game, all I can think about is getting that next hit of poison, even if I haven't made a single dollar from the business model yet. It's not about the money. It's about the poison. Give me a hit of perfect poison. Finding that poison is not as difficult as you might think. Just keep trying different poisons like you would try different video games until you find one that hits you perfectly. Remember the list of different poisons that I gave you earlier in the book? Try a few of them. Try YouTube for thirty days. You will either love it or hate it. Go with your feelings. Try blogging for thirty days. Try creating a handmade product line to sell. I have a free training on this to help you get started at FreeHandmadeTraining.com. Try selling a few products on Amazon from other companies. Or try selling a few products on eBay or Etsy. Try TikTok. Just keep trying different business models until something hits you just right. Do not worry about how you will make money from it, that comes later. Remember, audience first!

If you can try a platform that can build an audience and you like it, stick with it, obsess with it. Be reckless. Remember, if nine out of ten businesses fail, you just need to try ten to get one to succeed. By your 10th business, you will also learn a helluva lot more than you did with your first business and that will increase your chances of success. Be unashamedly the worst, so you can be the best later. I find that this is difficult to swallow for those who care a lot about their image. I never had friends growing up and I annoyed the few who would be my friends. Therefore, I did not care about my image a whole lot when getting into entrepreneurship. But I have found that those with a lot of friends must maintain an image and they have a hard time sacrificing some of those nights out and the perfect image that they have built up for years. Have you ever heard the saying, "It can take a lifetime to build up a reputation and five minutes to destroy it?" It's time to take those five minutes to destroy it to make this work. This does not mean you will no longer care about what your friends think. The books that talk about not caring cannot make you not care. In fact, it will probably always bug you that you can't properly explain to your family and friends why you have to do what you are doing. They will likely always judge you and will always feel as though what you are doing is wrong. That is because it is always easier to be a critic than to perform.

When you have spent four years of sixteen-hour days building everything up and then your family and friends say that they think you got lucky? That is when you've made it, and it will annoy the hell out of you. When they try to tell you what you are doing wrong and what you could do better, or they have a different idea for you, that will annoy you even more. Can you turn that off and not care? Nope. But you can distract yourself by building another product, business, or experience for your audience. Play another video game. I usually use that annoyance as fuel to build something else.

I have two childhood friends that I communicate with on Marco Polo. The other day they were laughing at how both of them were forced into being my friend when we were younger and what a loser I was when we first met. Fine. Let me make another million at your laughter. They are still my friends and

I hope they laugh again to fuel my next million. I don't mind. I'm used to being awful. My dad used to ask me almost every day of my teenage years, "Why can't you be more like Sammy McDonald?" That was one of the neighborhood girls. She was thinner than I would ever be and had better grades than I could ever get. I tried and failed living up to a perfect image my whole life.

So, by now, I have resolved to be awful and what I call ugly. Launch Ugly.

CHAPTER 14

Launch Ugly

The definition of **Launch Ugly** is this:

Adjective: unpleasant or repulsive, especially in appearance, during a product launch.

I extend this to also being deaf, **Launch Deaf**. The definition of launch deaf is this:

Adjective: unable to hear words or conversations, especially during a product launch.

And then there's **Launch Fear**. The definition of launch fear is this:

Noun: the irrational fear of total and undeniable failure of one's entire business and entire self-identity right before a product launch.

If you have never been Launch Ugly, Launch Deaf or you have never experienced Launch Fear, then you are not playing the video game right. You are not putting enough on the line, you have not gotten far enough into the video game, or you have yet to sacrifice enough…or, you have never launched, don't know how to launch, or you do not even know what a launch is. I find most business owners just put stuff up and hope it sells. Jeff Walker from Product Launch Formula calls this 'hope marketing.' We never want to just put stuff up and 'hope' it sells. We do not want to open a brick n mortar store and 'hope' people find out about it. Maybe they hear about it from a neighbor, drive by and stop, and just hope it succeeds.

It's the same thing with anything in business. If you are making something that you want people to know about, then you need to plan a proper launch. The difference between a proper launch and just posting stuff is that a proper launch is planned, themed, prepared for, and everything is ready before you actually launch. It's similar to the launch of a rocket. The astronauts are trained, the rocket is built by the best engineers, and there is a medical staff to check the astronauts weeks before a departure. You get the picture. You do not need a staff to launch but you need a proper marketing plan, and you need it before your launch. You need photos taken of your products and marketing materials made up. Videos, social media posts, emails must be taken care of. All of this is completed before you go live. You do not just go live and then figure it out. I mean you can but remember, that is hope marketing. When planning a launch, think of it like planning the biggest, coolest party ever for your product. It might be online, so you need to showcase it digitally. You will want awesome photographs taken, videos, and a theme to go with it. The theme is not the same as your branding. Your branding is consistent and your launch theme should tie in with your branding, obviously. But a launch theme can vary while branding stays the same.

The company that is the best at this is Tiffany & Co. If you ever sign up for their email list, you will see how they launch a new designer product line. Sometimes it revolves around a celebrity, or an art form. Other times, it simply adds a new color tied in with their famous Tiffany Blue. I have seen them tie in white for the holidays and pink for Valentine's Day. But these were not released on only one day. It is like fireworks as they slowly release until the grand finale. You never know or see all of the fireworks at once. You never know what is coming next. But when you see it, you love it. You know it goes with the brand and the current marketing campaign.

A marketing campaign and a launch campaign are interchangeable and mean the same thing. But a marketing campaign can go on continuously while a launch campaign is generally for something new such as a new product line, company or company division. Most business owners will spend all of their money on creating products that there is very little left in the budget for their main launch or their product line launch. They look for free online traffic and find there is very little left and they can't seem to gain success from it. They try to spend a dime to sell $3,000 worth of products when in reality, they should have thought of the marketing budget before creating the products or company in the first place. If you go to purchase any franchise, they tell you approximately how much it will cost for the products, renovations, leasing or purchasing the space and also…the marketing for your launch. Franchises allocate a bigger chunk than you can imagine for this, knowing it takes a lot of fuel to get a company off the ground.

The better you plan for your launch, the better your photographs and videos and the more professional you appear. Will you get more sales because of this planning, budgeting, and spending? Yes and no. Does a rocket ever get the fuel back from its initial launch? Nope. But does it eventually float in outer space and no longer need that fuel? Yep!

Results.

The more you plan and build before you launch, the more Launch Ugly and Launch Deaf you become. Also, the more Launch Fear you will have when it comes time to actually go live or open your doors, even if you know that the results will be little to no big deal. But still, you have to launch to get off the ground. Let me give you an example of a launch that led to zero sales but was critical to do it up and launch properly like a rocket anyway. I launched my first baby clothing collection called 'Coco Collection' on my website Pristus.com. I got everything ready for it. I had a professional photographer in California hire a mom, dad, and baby to model the clothing. We got a ton of footage and I paid a ton for the bill, $3500 to be exact. Afterward, I hired someone to design all the emails, a special logo just for the collection, and design all the social media that would go out for the next three months.

But here is the thing. Even if every single item from this collection sold, I would actually suffer a loss of $3100. When I launched, I sold less than $100 worth of clothing. So why would I do it this way? Why would I lose money…or fuel…on purpose like this?

2 reasons.

1. I was able to instantly establish myself as a baby clothing brand designer. Everyone who saw the photos, collection, website, our shop, saw me as serious, credible, and the authority in baby clothing. Period. Because of this, I will be able to use those photos and clothing collections for the next ten, twenty, or hundred years to show that we were right from the start, even before we sold anything. This makes you credible with media, magazines, and more importantly, future customers.
2. What came first, the chicken or the egg? What came first, the products or the customers? Right? You must launch products first and then bring in customers. But if you are looking to your customers and sales to make you credible, you will wait forever. Customers want to see your social proof, bling, trustworthiness, established brand, before they become your customers. So, even though I sold very little on my first product line, I would not sell very much more with my second, third, or fourth product lines if I don't show my customers what they are missing from the first product line. Every company has to start with zero. Zero customers, products, branding. You have to come

out of the gate with a bang. And a launch and a product line launch is that bang. No, you might not get many sales, but you will take off and eventually be floating in space.

From that product line collection launch I started learning things from the people seeing the collection who were not buying and also from those who were. I started collecting data about what they liked, did not like, if they were buying for themselves, babies or friends' babies. This will then make the next product line launch even more profitable and so on until we basically take up the entire American nation with our brand.

No launch? No brand.

And get this. Most people who launch, do not know what they are even doing. But that is okay. You are not going to have as much buzz, traffic, and sales as you would expect on your first launch. So, it is okay to be awful at your first and even tenth launch. It is okay to be Launch Ugly and have Launch Fear. I have received tens of thousands of emails from fans that say their number one fear is too much success too quickly. I hate to disappoint you. That is like saying you will brush your teeth on Friday and accidentally be a dentist by Monday. This video game takes a lot of work and fuel to get off the ground. But eventually, you can let it float after you automate things.

CHAPTER 15

Automate Ugly

How many times have you moved in your life? And if you knew you had to move every couple of years, would you set your home up differently? Buy less? I have moved every three years for my entire life except once, when my parents stayed in one house between my ages of 11 - 18. Other than that, either my parents moved every few years or I did too as an adult. Because of this, I have some crazy habits.

When Tom and I got together, we also started moving every couple of years. I just kept convincing him that we "needed" to. This time, he is determined to stay in the home we are in. We just hit the two-year mark and we will see what happens next year. I did not realize I had these weird habits of living until I married Tom though. I had this big box of photos and decor to hang on the walls. Yet, I never unpacked it because we might be moving again. So Tom decided he would do it. He put everything up. Then…we moved and had to take it all down. This time I am going to try to stay put and actually make plans in our current home.

Building and running a business or multiple businesses, can be the same as moving. If you have not moved, you probably never purged to the degree that you have to when you move. When you constantly move, you have your home systematized and you keep the moving boxes in the basement. It is the same when you have automated businesses before.

When I operated my first successful business, I ran out of gas and wanted to quit. Yes, I was making six-figures but I was working sixteen hours a day with three kids, two of them in diapers, and a non-existent husband at the time. I was tired. Then I read a book that talked about automation. Normally, this book would have been so boring that I would rather change diapers. But because of how tired I was, this book was a complete liberation. It was water in the desert. At first, I thought, I cannot automate my business. I have too many unique products with multiple variables, colors and accessories. How could I ever outsource that to someone? But I quickly learned that documenting was king. As I did something in my business, I documented it in a Word document or spreadsheet. And slowly but surely, my entire business was on paper. From there, I organized it and was able to train someone to run the whole business for me. It took a while to train her on the things I thought she could not be trained on. But eventually, she ran my entire business while I cleaned the toilets in my home, and I have never been so ecstatic to clean toilets. Because I had been working sixteen hours a day on my business, I pretty much wanted to do anything else. Ironically, it was the maid cleaning the toilets that I trained to run my business so that I could switch with her. She was as excited to stop cleaning toilets as I was to stop running my business. This automation process was time consuming and extremely messy. Kind of like moving if you have not moved in thirty years and never intended to.

But…The next business that I built I did so differently, with the automation in mind. I did not do everything first and then write it in the documents or spreadsheets. Instead, I started with the documents and spreadsheets as I built. This way, the business is automated as I go, and it is easier to hand it over when I am done. It is like building a big machine. No one but you could do the building, but anyone can run it when it is built. Burnout is the number one reason that successful businesses fail. It is run by someone who does not realize that they can hand it over. So, they run on a never ending treadmill until…they are legitimately exhausted. This chapter might not even apply to you right now, especially if you have never started a business. Imagine giving advice to a newlywed couple who serve in the air force though. You go to their wedding, and they tell you that they are going to buy a big ranch with horses, cows, ducks, and pigs and they plan to have twenty kids to go with it. Oh…And she is an artist while her husband is in the air force, so she is going to build a studio to the side of her house to paint in.

What would you think about this if you knew they could potentially be moving every three years? You might warn them that this might not be such a great idea…unless they have a tight system to move that entire set up anywhere in the world. Someone should make a farm setup just like the kid toys where it can fold up and move. They would make billions. Anyway, even if you haven't started a business yet, I am trying to warn you of a big mess coming if you do not document as you build. You do not even need to know exactly what you are doing or documenting. But as you build just think 'Would an employee someday need to access this information? Would they need me to explain this to them? Would someone potentially put this thing together someday?' If you say "yes" to any of these, then write down the process, take photos of what you do, how you do it, what you click, and the password to get in. And then, if you need to change that process, document it again. This is a total headache; I will not lie. Especially as you build and realize you have made mistakes and must change and document those changes. It feels like a total waste of time. But then, someone amazing walks in the door and you hand them the manual and say, "Good luck!" If you are an introvert, you will not even have to talk to them. And if they are an introvert, they will love you even more because they do not have to talk to you!

They know what to do and they can then train everyone else to do it too.

Again, there is no step by step to automation beyond recording your day-to -day business activity and making a manual where you can input all of that information for someone to read. It does not need to look pretty. It can be hideously ugly. Your fingers do not need to be manicured. Your computer screen does not need to be cleaned up.

Automate Ugly. Hey! That's a new one. After you Launch Ugly...Automate Ugly.

The definition of **Automate Ugly** is:

Adjective: unpleasant or repulsive, especially in company records and manuals, during a company's automation process.

CHAPTER 16

Pressure

I have bought many online courses and most of them talk about your 'why' and the reason it is important to know your 'why.' Your 'why' is your motivation behind starting, running, automating, and scaling your business.

Many coaches try to hit this subject first in a paid course so you can source your own motivation to get through the hard times you are about to experience while building. I used to think these sections were complete drivel unless you were a nutcase that needed such a section. I do not need a 'why.' I just enjoy the video games. Do you have to ask a gamer to think about their 'why' when a video game gets difficult? No! They are just frustrated that they cannot get beyond a certain part, and they have to keep going until they do. A gamer never passes a difficult level that took a lot of time and then wonders why they are not on level ten yet. They just wonder what the next level is like.

So, to me, the people who need their 'why' are probably the most likely to quit as they may have picked the wrong poison. They want the result without being addicted to the work. A 'why' will not get you through the pure hatred of the work. Having said this, I was recently going through a company crash, and I thought about quitting. I was trying to get my fever back and I eventually reached in the back of my head to see if my 'why' could motivate me back into a fever to get going again. I could not find it. My 'why' was lost. Finally, when I realized what my 'why' was, and not what I wanted it to be, I knew I could not use it. Underneath it all, my 'why' is shallow. I crave approval. I crave it like a drug, just like my video game.

I spent a quarter of a million dollars on my stepdaughter trying to get her approval and she cut me off when I cut the money off. Clearly, not everyone's love can be bought. But I tried just the same. My 'why' is actually a danger to my business as much as it is helpful. But I cannot change my 'why' just because I want to. Then it is not real. I had a staff of 27 people, and I was continuously planning launches for everyone to be paid. My staff started complaining about the launches. They said, "This is getting ridiculous" and asked, "Do we have to work so much?" My own assistant ordered me to only work eight hours a day, eat right and exercise because she was worried about my stress levels. Another assistant complained because I asked her to post something on Instagram and she said she wished I had given her more than a two week notice to post something onto our Instagram account.

Suddenly…my 'why' that had always been inside me, was gone. Because my 'why' was my staff's approval, I did not want to make them work, even though I knew it would lead to the company's demise. I thought, they will hate me if I make them launch again. My fever was instantly gone, and I crashed. I had no desire to launch anymore. Why am I going to pull teeth to launch further when they do not want to do the work? I sat and watched as the ship slowly went down. Finally, when we had two weeks left of everyone's pay, I let them know and laid everyone off. At that moment they all said, "Wait what? Can't we just do a launch?" But it was too late at that time. We needed to be launching all along for the numbers to continue to pay them.

You see, what they saw as unnecessary stress within me, was actually a very healthy self-pressure run by a desire to pay them and grow together. I wish my 'why' was something better like feeding my family. I think most people who say that is their 'why' do not really know their real 'why.' Your real 'why' is probably something that you do not want to admit out loud, like an unhealthy obsession with gaining people's approval. What a lame excuse for letting a company crumble to the ground. I know. But I cannot change the truth. I can only work with people who love the video game as much as me, even if they only pretend that they love it, I will gladly take it. Personality disorders, remember?

I have learned that pressure is probably the only difference between a video game and real life. The video game is fun, and you can pretend real life does not exist. But really, once you turn off the video game, you get a gauge of what is going on and how you are doing with it. Did your video game pay the bills this month? Did your video game pay for your kids Invisalign this month? Was your video game able to pay for your daughter's prom dress? How about your baby's formula and diapers? This is when you feel the pressure. It is that pressure which leads you to play the video game more, harder and faster to be able to do those things. The pressure fuels the video game, the video game fuels the pressure. It is a vicious cycle for sure. If you are the breadwinner or want to be, you know exactly what I am talking about. There is a pressure that comes with it that cannot be compared to anything else. I am not looking down on home makers but…if you are a homemaker and you burn the dinner, we end up having pizza. No big deal. If I fail, we do not have dinner and you are going to give me that disappointed look, be angry, or divorce me. The kids will also be hungry and sad at their failed breadwinner. It's a pressure that has crushed millions and is the number one reason for suicides. Pressure is not a gender thing. It is a 'person who pays all the bills alone' thing. The pressure can add up to the point that you feel like an elephant is sitting on your chest, you can't breathe. You are about to completely bust into a thousand pieces from the pressure and in that moment, you have to work through it and figure out the impossible. I suddenly understand Marvel characters a lot better. Let me tell you, it is hard to remember your 'why' in that moment of failure with pressure bearing down on you. You kind of want to quit and go on government assistance at that moment. Why are you working so hard and under all this pressure? Your head will tell you. Maybe we should just downsize so I do not have to feel so much pressure. Well, this is the moment where you realize your 'why' cannot be someone else's approval or appreciation. This is when the fever and the poison from the video game takes over your 'why.' Your 'why' is useless. The poison and video game addiction is everything. Not addicted? There is no 'why' on this planet that can compete against that pressure. 'Why' is an ice cream that falls to the sand on a windy day. Your addiction cannot be stopped. I was ready to quit and go on government assistance. I mean, my husband is disabled now. We can get disability and retire on everything else. So why don't I? My husband told me why. He told me I would go crazy. And he is right. Why would I go crazy? Because I have a sick addiction that cannot be cured. My 'why' might have started as the noble "I need to feed my family" but it was really people's approval and that crumbled. The only thing that saved me was my addiction to play again. The addiction is who I am and my identity more than anything else.

You need an addiction to a poison that will hold onto you forever. You do not need a 'why' if your poison has chosen and holds on to you. You are your poison's 'why'. That is all you need to get through the pressure. Instead of finding your 'why' try to find your poison and be your poison's 'why.' Then it is like Hotel California, and you can check out anytime you like but you can never leave.

CHAPTER 17

The Game Does Not Care About You

I remember working tirelessly during the first 100 YouTube videos that I ever recorded and edited. I broke my brain trying to put up videos that I thought others would enjoy. I made the mistake of assuming that if people subscribed to me and my channel that they cared about and supported me. So, I made videos about me. One day, I was a guest on a popular blog. I looked the following day and saw that fifty new people subscribed to my YouTube channel and joined my email list from that popular blog. I was ecstatic and that day I put up a video about how hard my life was while running a business. How badly I was struggling. I cried physical tears on the video and broke down sobbing saying, "I don't know if I can do this. One day later, all fifty of the new subscribers were gone. They unsubscribed. Then more tears came as I screamed at my computer. "What do you want from me?!?" I screamed out loud as my children looked at me like I was a freak.

I gave my most vulnerable self in the video that made them unsubscribe. When I finally came to the realization that nobody cares about me, I realized something else…they only care about themselves. This critical realization hurt like hell. I felt completely worthless. I felt as though I would have to be a complete slave to my audience and serve them only without serving myself at all. I would have to ask for nothing and give everything. I was broken at this thought. Isn't the whole point of becoming a YouTuber that you have people and fans that care about you? Clearly, I was mistaken about that. I had to decide at this moment. What do I want to do? Really it was not my decision. I did not have a choice. I did not want to go on. I did not want to be a YouTuber. But the poison chose me. I could not stop. So, every video from then on was with my audience in mind instead of myself. And it worked. They subscribed if they were being served. But I realized throughout the ten years that I have been YouTubing that someone who has been a fan for years is still willing to turn on me if I say one wrong thing and it bothers them. They say, "You're an idiot Renae! I've followed you for years and now I'm unsubscribing because you said that!" No matter what I do or say, there are comments like this with almost every video that I record. Even if you are not going to be a YouTuber, it is critical for you to realize that your game does not care about you. The audience that you serve, will not care about you. You need the philosophy of the audience first, but they will put you beyond last. They will abuse you, complain about you and they will give you horrible advice and rude social feedback. They will then call you greedy for serving them because you make a dollar from it.

After that, they will say that you are not paying enough taxes. And that you should run your business model as tight as Amazon so you can handle whatever the government decides to tax you on or new regulations that might bankrupt you. "You should know better!" They will tell you, after you have set up your entire business model, worked tirelessly for eighty hours a week to get your automation going with employees, and then a new regulation comes out that will destroy everything you worked to build. They will act like running a business is a solid industry with no risk if regulations and taxes are coming down the pike. Then they will refuse to invest in businesses when told that it can have the best ROI because it is too risky. Your consumers and audience will be a walking contradiction. It does not matter what you do or say, you will always be wrong, every time, no matter what. Everything you say or do also makes your fans assume that you have picked a political side. Even not picking a political side is picking a side. You are screwed no matter what. Your game does not care about you. But the sooner you accept this the better off you will be. Just master a resigned and defeated sigh. After that, realize that you will still have plenty of audience left over to pay the bills and support you. At least, until you tick them off too. Just keep serving them, polling them, and tweaking things to what they desire. You will get there eventually.

I once started a beach wedding invitation website. It got traffic, but nobody would buy my designs. I tried everything with seashells, color blocking, sand, wedding rings, beaches, ocean, palm trees, everything you could imagine that goes with a beach wedding. Still, nothing. Finally, after twelve months of launching ten new designs every week for the full 52 weeks, I finally found a design that sold well. It became a best seller and outsold any other invitation I had designed from any of my invitation websites. This design was a photograph of an empty beach, but it was in black and white. The water was a teal blue and that was the only color on the invitation. The invitation wording was directly on the water in white or black. Bam! How would I have ever known that from the start? It took me 520 invitation designs to make this one best seller that made me six figures over the next few years until I sold the business.

A lot of my YouTube followers launch one or two product lines, and they feel like a failure. Listen, after you have made 520 products, if you do not have one that sells well, you have my permission to quit. Otherwise, keep trying, keep playing the video game. The video game will not care about you. But if you pick the right poison, it also will not let you go.

So, enjoy those 520 levels to the top!

CHAPTER 18

Be The Thorn

Obviously, hacking websites and putting them up for ransom is wrong…and illegal. But sometimes the best way to make money is by being what the big corporations cannot be. Big corporations have a titanic sized ship to run. They must have big meetings to discuss every business decision, large or small. Instead of competing against that, be the virus that infects it. Obviously do not be an illegal virus.

Did you ever watch Disney's "Sword in the Stone"? The wizard Merlin combats the Mad Madam Mim. They both change into bigger and bigger animals until Mad Madam Mim becomes the biggest fire breathing dragon and it appears to be over. What could Merlin become that could be bigger than a dragon? Instead, he goes small. He becomes a virus that is so small enabling him to go undetected. Mad Madam Mim becomes sick, and the duel is over. Wizard Merlin wins. The corporations are the dragon.

You are the virus. They cannot move as quickly as you. They cannot even see you because you are so small. Find ways of taking their business. How would one go about doing this? Sales funnels are the virus that infects corporations. Corporations are too established to focus on sales funnels. Instead, corporations focus on lead generation through affiliate software like Rakuten, Honey and BeFrugal. Those software's can mean big bucks if they recommend you, but they only work with bigger companies. Not with you. So, you must swipe customers in a different way. Corporations have unlimited budgets. Your budget is nearly non-existent. We must do things a bit differently. We must do smart things. I have learned to do this through funnels or pipelines. Let me explain.

How does a funnel work in baking? There is a big top and a small bottom. You put something in the top and it drips down to the bottom. A sales funnel works the same way. You tap into traffic and as people start going through your funnel, people will drop out at different points, but the drip at the bottom are paid customers who will buy from you repeatedly.

You can capture people into your funnel several ways. You need:

1. A traffic source
2. Bait
3. Something to offer (free or paid)
4. Your own Renae Christine experience to warm them up until you sell them something else.

Remember that your traffic source can change as society changes.

Remember Myspace? Yikes. Google SEO used the number one way to get traffic. Now you must have a lot of dollars to pay a whole SEO team to do that. Then it became Facebook and Instagram Ads. They are still alright but when Apple turned off Facebook tracking, the whole business world panicked and looked for an alternative. Marketplaces can be a traffic source. For example, you can sell something on Amazon and include a link to a free product with the product delivery to capture them. YouTube ads also seem to be the big thing right now. But tomorrow, those traffic sources might change. It all depends on where your audience spends most of their time and that changes too. But if you have the rest of the steps set up, then it is just a matter of tapping your audience like you tap oil.

A sales pipeline is like a funnel in that it takes a customer from the start of your experience and brings them through to a sale. For example, a YouTuber might offer a free cheat sheet in exchange for an email. Then that YouTuber sends them several emails with great content. Then, after seven days, that YouTuber sends an email about an awesome product that they offer along with a unique, one time discount code that will expire in two days. This whole sales pipeline is automated and part of the experience. But you can see why it is called a pipeline. Once you are in the pipe, you cannot really escape unless you completely break free. And when people like you enough to sign up for your email list or make a purchase, they have a hard time breaking up with you because they might miss something important in the future.

I once abandoned my email list for a year and a half. During this time, I got together with other business partners, and they emailed my list from them. After a year and a half, I canceled the program to reclaim my list because of many complaints and requests for me to return. After I returned, I got emails and messages from fans that said they never opened a single email from my partners, and they waited the entire time for me to return without unsubscribing. They would not unsubscribe because they feared that I might return, and they would not know about it. So, they just let the emails go unread from my partners until I came back.

There goes my theory that your audience does not care about you. Some do, I guess. And when they do, that is when you want to absolutely spoil them silly with a new Renae Christine Experience.

CHAPTER 19

My Only Rule For Myself

We've gone over fifteen years of everything I have learned as an entrepreneur up until now. There is a chance that I may have confused you more than helped you. Here is one of the first, most unconfusing things that I have learned and that is the only rule that I ultimately live by. If I live by this one rule, I can be as reckless as I want in my business adventures and somehow it always works out in the end. I learned this a while back from an investing book that I read. That book was more about investing in real estate and I thought there was no true adventure in that. But still, I learned this one rule that made the difference for myself over the course of all these years. I have already sat my kids down and taught it to them as well. It is truly the rule that makes people rich, wealthy, long-term wealthy, and provides generational wealth. It is the one rule that nobody seems to believe or listen to. It's the one rule that I think about when someone tells me that "I'm spending too much or I'm over-extending myself financially."

This is the true financial literacy rule that, if they taught this in academia, everyone would learn how to truly be wealthy. And it is so very simple. But I think most people get impatient or they just do not believe in it. However, here is the rule.

Make Money -> Feed An Asset -> That Asset Makes Money -> Pay The Bills With The Money The Asset Made. Period.

Every time a person makes a financial decision, or the government makes a spending decision, I think of this rule. Every time the government wants to pull more taxes from people or businesses, instead of investing money in more American factories and manufacturers, I think of this rule. Every time someone who doesn't know this rule says "Hello! Economics 101!" who thinks the stock market has anything to do with the real wealth of the economy, I think of this rule, and that they are a bit stupid. This rule sounds so simple, yet nobody follows it. After teaching my sixteen-year-old daughter this rule, she made the decision to skip college, and instead, save up her money to buy the franchise business of her dream. A college degree is not an asset that makes money. You might be turning yourself into an asset by building skills, but my daughter wants an asset that makes money for her instead of herself being the asset. She made this decision on her own after learning this rule. That is smart.

I bet if you polled college graduates who have worked longer than twenty years in their industries and asked them if they would have rather taken their college payment and sunk it into a business franchise, if they would have done it. I am confident that most of them would say, "Yes." I know that my generation went to college mostly because our parents thought it was the only way to make real money. My family still believes college is the best way. My mom has a college degree. My dad has a college degree. My family is not wealthy. How many college graduates are wealthy? They work for the wealthy.

The other day, my sixteen-year-old daughter said to me that "CEOs read an average of sixty books a year." She was impressed and immediately wanted to pick up sixty books. "CEOs," I responded, "are hired by us." I could see the lightbulb turn on in her head as this sentiment resonated with her. Was that a rude thing to say? I am not looking down on CEOs but if you are looking to get wealthy, you must change your mindset a little bit. College degrees train people to work for us. You too, reading this. CEOs work for you. Maybe not right now, but soon after you play the video game long enough, they will.

I am not looking down on people with college degrees. I was sucked into the college degree dream, and I spent five years getting my bachelor's degree. But afterward, I didn't use it. I got a little bit sidetracked when I got sucked into a business video game. This rule of mine, it makes the business video game even more fun because spending is okay. The more you spend, the more your asset makes and the bigger house you can afford. Let me paint a visualization of my rule so you can better see how it works in practice.

Let's say John has a job. He gets paid $12/hour after taxes. After 40 hours of work, John has $480 in his bank account. This is John's first job. He wants to save money to buy a car and insurance, a phone, as well as a home. Instead, he lives with his parent(s) and saves every penny to buy a franchise. After one year, he has $24,960 in his bank account. After five years, he has $124,800 in his bank account. The franchise he wants to buy requires $120,000 liquid capital up front. John has it. During those five years, John also took some side jobs so that he could buy a few fun things for himself. He opened a few credit cards to build credit during that time. He paid off his credit cards every month. After five years, John now has the liquid capital and the credit needed to start his franchise. The franchise that he chose provides the training needed to run the franchise successfully. The franchise also holds John's hand through each step of building the franchise. The franchise also has all the contacts, sourcing, products, name, marketing and everything needed to run the business successfully. The franchise prefers to work with people like John who are willing to work within their rules instead of getting their own ideas which might fail the franchise business. After another year of building out the franchise, John launches and immediately takes in a six-figure salary. John now makes $100,000 a year while his friends, coming out of college, make $35,000 starting wage. John immediately uses his salary from his franchise asset to buy a car, phone and a home. John would be pretty much set for life because he chose to get a job, invest that job's money into an asset, and then pay the bills with that asset. Real estate can be an asset, but John finds that boring.

He is more interested in business. So, for his first business, he cut his teeth through a franchise to get all of the training that he needed. If John no longer enjoys being run by the franchise corporation, he can sell it and spend that money on another company that he owns and can run with his own ideas. I am not telling you to go out and buy a franchise. But I am telling you to get money through a job, spend that money on an asset, not bills. When that asset starts making money, that is the money you spend on bills. It is difficult to swallow because, who wants to save their money for five years to buy an asset, especially when they are only sixteen? It might be even harder for someone who just turned forty and already has bills. But, I will tell you this. I believe in this principle so strongly that, even if I lost everything, I would get two jobs, live within the means of one job, even if it meant moving in with someone or living in a studio apartment with four kids and a husband for five years in order to build up and buy another asset again to pay the bills of a bigger home.

This ultimate money-making principle is what makes the video game work. It is what makes it possible for you to crash as many times as you need and still make money. It is the lack of this principle that makes celebrities lose everything they obtain. It is the lack of this principle that took that person that I knew, whose father left them $500,000 and they lost it all and ended up living in a trailer. Get money and pay your bills? You will likely struggle all of your life. Get money and get an asset then pay your bills? You will be set all of your life. This is the ultimate principle that makes the cliche "it takes money to make money" work but most of the people who say that assume they need more money than they are making to make money. As if it takes some large sum of a million dollars to make more than that. Like the money comes with financial literacy and a knowledge of what to do. I once listened to this radio show where people could call in and pretend that they won the lottery. The host said, "pretend you just won a million dollars in the lottery. What would you do with it?" Every single one of them said *that they would pay off their house and bills and then spend the rest on friends and family or save the rest.* Guess what? They would all end up broke because of my principle.

First, the government would take half. So, you only have $500,000 left. Ironically, this is exactly the figure the person I knew ended up with when her father passed away. And she did exactly what everyone on that radio show said they would do. She bought a house and paid her bills. She now lives in a trailer. If she would have taken that money and purchased an asset such as a company or real estate, she could be fine to this day. She could have made real wealth. Sometimes I check out Reddit and listen to poor people talk about how to make money. They all think they know, and they will even talk about this ultimate money-making principle. And then in the next breath they talk about the big television that they bought with their tax return. Usually, people believe in my favorite rule, but they do not live by it.

More people usually live this way:

Get a job -> pay bills -> save money -> anything extra can be saved for an asset.

There's no money left this way and it can't generate wealth. This is a spiral downward instead of upward. These are the people that think they're living by the rule because they have a mortgage, and they feel that their home is their greatest asset. A home is a great asset, but it is not a money-making asset that can help you pay the bills. This is the difference. You need a money-making asset. You need to invest in something that makes dollar bills come out at the end. You need to buy a machine where, if you put in $1, $2 comes out. How many people would save to buy a machine like that before paying the bills? Everyone would buy a machine like that! But they don't. And I am not really sure of the reason why. Maybe they think they will do something like that later on. Or maybe they have a spouse that would divorce them if they had to downsize in order to start saving for the machine. Or maybe they do not really believe it will work. Maybe the machine will break. Maybe they will only lose money. After all, it is a risk, right?

Let me tell you something. If I lose it all, I can still build it back up again. And I have, twice. This is the difference between living by my rule versus not doing so. This one rule means I can go for broke in my assets and if I lose, I just play the video game again and eventually I will hit three cherries on the slot machine to redeem myself. When I taught this to my kids, they asked me, "what is a money-making asset?" I explained, "any asset where money comes out at the end of it and it can be automated to not require your time." One easy example, a vending machine. That is an obvious money-making asset, and you can multiply them until you can hire out restocking the machines. The stock market with stocks that pay dividends. To me that is such slow money that it makes me want to drown myself. But it is for some people, and it is an asset that makes money come out on the other end. A rental property, business or personal, is a money-making asset. People pay rent. A percentage of that rent goes in your pocket each month to pay the bills. Some people say this is the safest investment, but I have fifteen years of business experience, so, for me, a rental property would actually be more of a risk than going with what I know. Also, what a boring video game. But it might be for you. A franchise business is an asset. Possibly less risky than trying to build a business yourself. My kid chose this because it will train her as well. I cannot train my kids beyond the basics. I am too busy playing the video game to stop and explain it. An online business asset. This can also be risky, but you can acquire one that pretty much runs itself from Empire Flippers. They have cheaper assets than a franchise and it might be less risky as they almost always run themselves. Of course, remember that it is a video game and there is risk with everything. You are rolling the dice but if you do not roll the dice, you can never win big.

If you're just starting out, I would suggest getting an asset with Empire Flippers because it is like buying that machine where you put in $1 and you make $2. It is already all set up and usually has an employee or two that comes with it. Also, if you are a newbie, Empire Flippers can help you pick something out that you cannot screw up.

You can also choose a 'Done For You' business asset, where you can pay an experienced business coach and team to build something for you that works and makes money. I did this with Seth Kniep's Amazon FBA Done For You Program. This can make a lot of dollars come out, but it is probably the most risky of all and takes a few years to build out. It also costs as much as an Empire Flippers asset that makes money on day 1. Listen though, before running out and buying any asset, try the poison first. This is important. You have to like the poison. The poison has to choose you. You must get an uncontrollable fever while working the day to day in running that asset. I am not talking about getting a fever about the money that's going to come out. You have to get a fever for work. You have to get a fever for the video game itself, not the coins in the video game. You cannot care about the coins. You have to like the game itself. My kid got hired at the franchise she wants to purchase so she can train from the bottom up to eventually run it. This is far more valuable than my daughter going to college for a business degree. She is being paid for the education she truly needs to run the place. And she will be able to see if it really is her poison before purchasing it. She will know if this is really her poison or if she needs to try something else.

All of this might sound overwhelming, risky, and maybe you do not know where to start. Just like ice cream, you have to taste the different flavors before making a decision. So, dip in, grab a course or two, and start trying different things before making an ultimate decision. Do not worry about wasting money. This is the exact money you should be spending to get what you really want. If I went bankrupt and had to start over, this is exactly what I would do to build it back up. Remember, if you don't live by this rule, you will never get that shot. You are not even playing in the game. You cannot win if you do not recklessly play.

Are you ready to play yet?

CPSIA information can be obtained
at www.ICGtesting.com
Printed in the USA
LVHW011919210921
698350LV00006B/61/J

9 781953 607232